A-LEVEL
STUDENT GUIDE

OCR

Physical Education

Psychological factors affecting performance

Michaela Byrne

HODDER
EDUCATION
AN HACHETTE UK COMPANY

This Student Guide has been written specifically to support students preparing for the OCR A-level Physical Education examinations. The content has been neither approved nor endorsed by OCR and remains the sole responsibility of the author.

Hachette UK's policy is to use papers that are natural, renewable and recyclable products and made from wood grown in well-managed forests and other controlled sources. The logging and manufacturing processes are expected to conform to the environmental regulations of the country of origin.

Orders: please contact Bookpoint Ltd, 130 Park Drive, Milton Park, Abingdon, Oxon OX14 4SE. Telephone: (44) 01235 827827. Fax: (44) 01235 400401. Email: education@bookpoint. co.uk. Lines are open from 9 a.m. to 5 p.m., Monday to Saturday, with a 24-hour message answering service. You can also order through our website: www.hoddereducation.co.uk.

ISBN 978-1-5104-7209-9

First printed 2020

First published in 2020 by
Hodder Education,
An Hachette UK Company
Carmelite House
50 Victoria Embankment
London EC4Y 0DZ

www.hoddereducation.co.uk

Impression number 10 9 8 7 6 5 4 3 2 1

Year 2023 2022 2021 2020

Cover photo: ohishiftl/Adobe Stock

Typeset by Integra Software Services Pvt. Ltd, Pondicherry, India

Printed in Italy

A catalogue record for this title is available from the British Library.

MIX
Paper from
responsible sources
FSC™ C104740

Contents

Content Guidance

Questions & Answers

■ Getting the most from this book

Exam tips

Advice on key points in the text to help you learn and recall content, avoid pitfalls, and polish your exam technique in order to boost your grade.

Knowledge check

Rapid-fire questions throughout the Content Guidance section to check your understanding.

Knowledge check answers

1 Turn to the back of the book for the Knowledge check answers.

Summaries

- Each core topic is rounded off by a bullet-list summary for quick-check reference of what you need to know.

Exam-style questions

Commentary on the questions

Tips on what you need to do to gain full marks.

Sample student answers

Practise the questions, then look at the student answers that follow.

Commentary on sample student answers

Read the comments showing how many marks each answer would be awarded in the exam and exactly where marks are gained or lost.

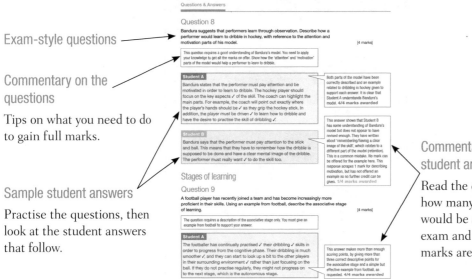

■About this book

This Student Guide covers the topics required for OCR A-level specification H555 Paper 2: Psychological factors affecting performance. Remember that this is a guide, not a textbook. It provides a summary of what you need to know and understand for your exam, but is intended to complement, not replace, your textbook and class notes.

The Content Guidance section follows the headings set out in the OCR specification. It is divided into two main topics:
■ Skill acquisition
■ Sports psychology

Use the knowledge checks as you progress through each topic to test your understanding, and take on board the exam tips in order to avoid falling into the traps that most commonly result in students losing marks. At the end of each topic area there is an overall summary of the content covered — if you are unable to offer a detailed explanation of any part of this, you should work through this section again to clear up any misunderstanding.

The Questions & Answers section begins by setting out the format of the exam papers, giving you advice and important tips on how to maximise your marks on the different elements of the paper. It also explains the levels system used for extended questions.

This is followed by a series of sample questions. After each of these questions there are some example answers from students illustrating both best practice as well as not such good practice. You should attempt all of these questions yourself and compare your answers with the example answers while reading the detailed comments to help improve your understanding of what is required to achieve top marks.

Content Guidance

■ Skill acquisition

By studying skill acquisition, you will develop knowledge and understanding of how sporting skills are acquired and enhanced. Performing skills to a high level is something that is acquired or learned, rather than being natural or innate.

You will learn how to classify skills on a variety of continua and therefore understand the most effective way of presenting these skills to learners and how to practise them to perfection. An understanding of how the performer's experience of one skill can affect the learning and performance of another will be developed through this area.

You will understand how environmental conditions affect the acquisition and development of sporting skills and be able to suggest the most effective methods for each. By understanding methods of guidance, you will be able to suggest ways in which performers can be supported when learning sporting skills. Knowledge of the types of feedback will enable you to motivate performers and correct their errors. Different psychological approaches will be studied that suggest how skills are learned and the stages of learning that performers pass through.

Most importantly, you will be able to apply the knowledge you have gained to sporting skills and situations. Whether you are a performer, leader or coach in sport, this psychological knowledge will enhance your role.

Classification of skills

A continuum is an imaginary sliding scale on which skills can be placed between two extremes. Continua are used to classify and group skills together and to show variations in characteristics. It is important to understand the characteristics of skills so that they can be taught, practised and perfected. You must have knowledge and understanding of the six continua below and be able to *justify* your positioning of skills on each of them.

Difficulty

This continuum classifies skills based on the amount of information to process and, as a result, the level of decision-making and perception/judgement required to produce the skill.

- **Simple skills** — there is little information to process and therefore few decisions and limited use of perception/judgement are required to produce the skill. It usually involves one action that can be taught as a whole, for example a leap in dance.
- **Complex skills** — there is a large amount of information to process, meaning that several decisions and lots of judgements are made by the performer when producing the skill. The skill is often open, and requires the performer to adapt to

the surrounding environment. For example, when passing in basketball, the player considers who to pass to and the type of pass, and also makes a judgement on the required power and trajectory of the pass.

Environmental influence

This continuum classifies skills based on the effect of the environment/situation the performer is in on the production of the skill.

- **Open skills** — the environment is ever-changing and unpredictable. The performer must adapt, make lots of decisions and use their perception. Skills are often externally paced: for example, when passing in hockey the player adjusts to the position of their own players as well as those of the opposition.
- **Closed skills** — the environment is stable and predictable, allowing the performer to repeat the same movement pattern over and over without adjusting. The skill can be produced habitually and is often self-paced: for example a javelin throw.

Pacing

This continuum classifies skills based on how much control the performer has on the timing and speed of the movement.

- **Self-paced skills** — the performer controls the timing and speed of the skill: for example, a gymnast decides when and how quickly to perform a cartwheel.
- **Externally paced skills** — the environment controls the timing and speed of the skill being performed: for example, a kite surfer responds to wind speed and direction in order to gain big air.

Muscular involvement

This continuum classifies skills based on the muscles and precision required to produce the skill.

- **Gross skills** — these are performed using large muscle groups and a low level of precision: for example, a rugby tackle utilises large muscle groups, such as the quadriceps.
- **Fine skills** — these are performed with small muscle groups and require precision, accuracy and control: for example, pistol shooting uses small muscles in the arm and needs the performer to be exact with their aim.

Continuity

This continuum classifies skills based on the clarity of the start and end of the movement, and on how closely linked the subroutines are.

- **Discrete skills** — these have a clear beginning and ending. The skill is a single action — the performer must start at the beginning each time they perform the skill. For example, an overhead clear in badminton is a swift action that has an easily identifiable start and finish.
- **Serial skills** — here a number of discrete skills are grouped together and performed in a specific order, for example performing the hop, step and jump sequentially as the triple jump.
- **Continuous skills** — these do not have a clear beginning and ending — the skills are cyclic. The end of one skill becomes the beginning of the next and it is difficult to identify individual subroutines, for example cycling.

Subroutines The individual parts that are grouped together sequentially to make up the full skill.

Organisation

This continuum classifies skills based on how closely the subroutines are linked and whether the performer can practise each subroutine in isolation.

- **High-organisation skills** — these are hard to break down into subroutines and practise individually because the subroutines are closely linked. Therefore, the performer has to practise the skill as a whole. They are often ballistic, for example a sprint start.
- **Low-organisation skills** — these are easy to separate into subroutines that can be practised individually. For example, in the breaststroke the arm action and leg kick can be isolated and practised separately until grooved/overlearned.

Ballistic Fast, dynamic and powerful movements.

Grooved/overlearned Practised to perfection.

Exam tip

Questions on classification appear regularly on exam papers. Focus clearly on the command verb: you will be asked to *justify* your answer, that is, give a reason. Use 'because' in your answer and always support it with a practical example.

When choosing a practical example to illustrate your answer, ensure that it is towards the extremity of the continuum so it is clear to the examiner where your skill is placed.

Knowledge check 1

What are the continuity and difficulty skills classification continua based on?

Summary

After studying this topic you should be able to:
- name and describe each of the continua — difficulty (simple or complex), environmental influence (open or closed), pacing (self-paced or externally paced), muscular involvement (gross or fine), continuity (discrete or serial or continuous) and organisation (high organisation or low organisation)
- label and describe the extremes of the continua and support this with clear practical examples at each end, ensuring that you name the skills and not just the sports involved
- justify your reasons for classifying skills on each of the continua

Types and methods of practice

When learning a skill, it is important to grasp its classification before deciding how to present and practise it. For example, coaches should consider the organisation and complexity of the skill, the level of danger involved and the clarity of the start and end of the skill. The environment should also be taken into consideration.

Knowledge check 2

What should a coach consider before deciding which practice method to use?

Part practice

When using part practice, the coach presents the skill in parts/sections/subroutines. Each subroutine can be practised individually and grooved before practising the full skill.

This method should be used when the skill is low organisation and/or serial, so the subroutines are easily distinguishable from each other. The part method is also effective if the skill is complex and requires a high level of decision-making. It can also be used with dangerous skills, where practising the parts rather than the whole skill will reduce the risk of injury.

If a performer is in the cognitive stage of learning, this method should be used so that they do not become overloaded. It can also be used if the performer is lacking in

Cognitive stage The first stage of learning. The performer is a novice, tending to be uncoordinated and making several mistakes.

motivation, because they only need to concentrate on succeeding in one subroutine/ part. If a more experienced performer is having difficulty with a specific subroutine, the part method can also be used to focus on grooving that aspect of the skill before integrating it into the full skill.

For example, the part method can be used with a ten-bounce routine in trampolining. The performer should practise each of the components individually — tuck jump, swivel hips, back drop, etc. — until it is grooved. Once each component is grooved, the performer should move on to learn the next component. Finally, they should practise the full routine including all the parts that have been grooved.

Advantages

- Confidence and motivation increase as success is experienced in each part/ subroutine.
- By focusing on one subroutine at a time it reduces the chance of information overload and fatigue, aiding understanding of each subroutine/part.
- Danger is reduced.

Disadvantages

- It is time-consuming.
- It cannot be used with highly organised skills because they are difficult to separate into subroutines.
- The fluency between subroutines can be negatively affected as parts are practised individually.
- **Kinaesthesis**/feel for the whole skill is not experienced until the end, which can restrict how it feels to perform.
- The performer may lose motivation because they are not performing the full skill until the end of the process.

Kinaesthesis The internal, muscular sensation of the movements being carried out.

Whole practice

When using this method, the coach presents the skill in its entirety. The skill is not broken down into parts/subroutines. For example, the whole method can be used when learning a golf swing, cycling or forward roll, each of which can be presented in one action.

This method should be used when the skill is highly organised and/or continuous, because the skill is difficult to separate into subroutines that can be practised individually. It is effective if the skill is simple and requires few decisions to be made. It can also be used with discrete skills, where the beginning and end of the skill is clear, and if it is fast/ballistic. This method is also appropriate if the skill presents no danger.

Autonomous performers can be successful when using this method because they are able to process all of the information relating to the skill.

Autonomous When the performer is in the final stages of learning. Their movements are accurate and fluent, and they have well-developed motor programmes.

Advantages

- It includes the development of kinaesthesis — the performer is able to 'feel' the full skill when performing it in its entirety.
- The fluency between the subroutines is maintained.
- It is not time-consuming.

- The performer can develop a clear mental image of the full skill and, because it is performed fully, the performer understands it and can more easily transfer it into a full game situation.

Disadvantages

- It can cause information overload and is therefore difficult to use with cognitive performers.
- It can cause fatigue.
- The performer must be physically capable of producing the full skill — if they are not, this can lead to demotivation.

Whole-part-whole practice

When using this method, the learner attempts the full skill, and then one (or each) subroutine is practised in isolation, before it is integrated back into the entire skill, which is finally practised in full. This method should be used when the skill is low in organisation and/or serial because the parts/subroutines can be isolated.

For example, the whole-part-whole method can be used when swimming front crawl. The coach begins by introducing the full stroke, allowing the performer to experience it entirely. If the coach then notes that the arm action is weak, the performer will then practise the arm action in isolation, with the aid of a pull buoy/floats, until it is grooved. Finally, the performer will practise the full stroke as one again, now with improved arm action as a result of the part practice.

Advantages

- Weak parts/subroutines can be isolated and improved in the part-practice stage.
- Kinaesthesis is maintained in the whole stages. Therefore, the performer's confidence and motivation increase when they are successful in learning each part.
- Fluency between the subroutines is maintained in the whole-practice stages.

Disadvantages

- It is ineffective with highly organised skills because they cannot be separated into parts.
- Kinaesthesis and fluency can be negatively affected if the part is not integrated adequately and quickly into the full skill.
- It is more time-consuming than using the whole method.

Progressive-part practice

When using this method the coach isolates and teaches the first subroutine/part. The performer will practise until it is perfected. The subsequent parts/subroutines are isolated, practised and added sequentially until the whole of the skill can be performed. This is sometimes called '**chaining**'.

This method should be used when the skill is low-organisation and/or serial and can be easily separated into subroutines. It is beneficial to use this method with complex skills because it reduces the need to make several decisions at once. Safety can be maintained if this method is used with dangerous skills. It should be used readily with cognitive performers because it reduces the chance of information overload.

Chaining When a skill is separated into its subroutines and then, gradually, links/subroutines in the chain are added in sequence.

For example, the progressive-part method can be used when learning a triple jump. The coach should first introduce the 'hop' subroutine, and the performer will practise this until it is grooved. Then the 'step' is presented and practised until it is grooved. The hop and step are then practised together and grooved. The 'jump' is then presented and practised until it is grooved. Finally, the hop and step and jump are practised together until grooved.

Advantages
- Focusing on just one subroutine reduces the chance of overload and fatigue, and aids the understanding of each part.
- The performer's confidence and motivation increases as success is seen in each part.
- Danger is reduced.

Disadvantages
- It is time-consuming.
- It is difficult to use with highly organised skills because these are hard to separate into subroutines.
- As subroutines are practised individually and then chained, the fluency between the subroutines can be negatively affected, causing the skill to be 'jerky' and the performer to look uncoordinated.
- The kinaesthesis/feel for the whole skill is not experienced until the end.

Massed practice

The performer practises continuously without rest periods. This method should be used when the skill is discrete and has a clear beginning and ending. It can also be used with closed skills that are unaffected by the environment and with self-paced skills in which the performer is able to control the rate and timing of the skill. The limited demand on decision-making means that simple skills can be practised using this method.

This method can be used if a performer is in the autonomous stage of learning. It is also effective if they are highly motivated and physically fit due to the absence of rest periods.

For example, massed practice can be used when learning a badminton short serve. The performer can perfect the shot by repeatedly performing the action without rest.

Advantages
- Fitness can be improved during practice.
- Fatigue in the game situation can be simulated.

Disadvantages
- This method causes fatigue, so the performer may not be physically capable of undertaking the practice.
- There is no time for feedback.

Distributed practice

When using this method, the performer undertakes physical practice and intersperses this with rest periods. The rest periods may be used to undertake activity that is completely unrelated to the task in hand or simply to recover.

This method should be used when the skill is continuous; the rest periods will allow the performer to recover from the constant action. Using this with complex skills will assist in the decision-making process. It can be used with serial and/or low-organisation skills because feedback on each subroutine can be given. Rest periods are also useful when learning dangerous/tiring skills. Finally, this method can be used with externally paced and open skills.

For example, distributed practice can be used by a steeplechaser who runs part of the course during a training session, followed by a rest period. During rest they can mentally rehearse their run, visualising their stride pattern, and clearing the hurdles and water barriers.

Advantages

- It is effective with cognitive performers because the rest periods can be used to allow them to recover and receive feedback, enabling them to develop.
- Unfit performers and those lacking in motivation will benefit from the rest.
- Mental practice/visualisation can be undertaken in the rest periods. Using both mental and physical practice methods together is more effective than massed practice alone.

Disadvantages

- It can be time-consuming and cause motivational issues if the rest periods are too long.
- If there are a lot of people in the group, lengthy rest periods may result in poor behaviour and lack of discipline/focus.

Fixed practice

With this method the performer practises the same skill in a stable environment. The skill is repeated over and over without adjustments. For example, a gymnast repeatedly performs a cartwheel on a gym mat until it is perfected.

This method should be used when the skill is closed and is therefore unaffected by the environment. It can be used with simple skills because the decision-making element is low. Fixed practice can also be used if the skill is self-paced.

Advantages

- It is effective with autonomous performers who need to correct a specific skill/subroutine.
- Cognitive performers can use it if they wish to develop a **motor programme**.
- It is an effective method for motivated individuals.
- It grooves/overlearns the skill so that it becomes habitual.
- It is time efficient.

> **Exam tip**
>
> You must refer to a specific sporting skill in your answer rather than simply identifying the sport. For example, use 'when tackling in rugby' rather than just 'in rugby'.

> **Motor programme** A generalised movement pattern that is stored in the long-term memory after a lengthy period of practice.

Disadvantages

- The performer may find it monotonous and lose motivation.
- The performer may experience fatigue.
- As the skill is performed in a single, stable environment it is difficult to transfer into a full competitive game situation.

Varied practice

The performer practises skills and drills in a constantly changing environment. One skill can be developed through undertaking drills that become progressively more difficult.

This method is useful for open skills because the environment is constantly changing, and this practice method reflects that. It can also be used for externally paced and complex skills. For example, a netball goal attack practises shooting on goal from a range of positions in the circle. A passive defender is then introduced before progressing onto a fully active defender. Finally, the shot is practised in a conditioned or small-sided game.

Advantages

- It is effective with cognitive performers because they gradually develop a range of experiences that can be transferred into a fully competitive game situation.
- If a performer is lacking in motivation, varied practice offers a range of activities that will engage them more than fixed practice.
- It develops schemas and enables the positive transfer of skills from training into the game situation.

Disadvantages

- It is a time-consuming method and may also cause fatigue.
- There is a possibility of information overload if too many drills are presented at once.
- It can cause negative transfer.

Exam tip

Exam questions may ask you to describe the types of practice or compare them. You will also be asked which methods to use with different types of skills. Make sure you give specific skill examples rather than just naming the sports involved.

Knowledge check 3

Name the eight types of practice.

Summary

After studying this topic you should be able to:

- name and describe each method of practice — part, whole, whole-part-whole, progressive-part, massed, distributed, fixed and varied
- suggest which skill classifications (difficulty, environmental influence, pacing, muscular involvement, continuity and organisation) and performers (cognitive, associative or autonomous) are most appropriate for each method
- apply each practice type to a practical skill, giving a clear practical example of when you would utilise each practice method and making sure you clearly identify a specific skill rather than just the name of a sport

Transfer of skills

Transfer explains the effect that the learning and performance of one skill may have on the learning and performance of another. Nearly all learning is based on some form of transfer. Having knowledge and understanding of the classification of skills and the ways to practise them will assist teachers/coaches who decide to use transfer with their performers.

Types of transfer

Positive transfer

This type of transfer means that the learning and performance of one skill *helps* the athlete to learn and perform another skill. It often occurs when the movement patterns/subroutines of a skill are the same/similar to those of another skill. For example, learning the chest pass in basketball will assist the performer when they are learning the netball chest pass. In addition, the more the practice conditions can replicate the full, competitive situation, the more likely it is that positive transfer will occur. This is known as the **identical elements theory**. This type of transfer is effective for cognitive and associative performers, especially when the teacher/coach highlights which subroutines are similar in each of the skills.

Negative transfer

This type of transfer means that the learning and performance of one skill *hinders* the athlete when learning and performing another skill. For example, negative transfer occurs between tennis and badminton backhand skills. Performers may believe that because there are several obvious similarities between the games, such as both being net games that require a court and racket, the need for hand–eye coordination and similar tactics being used, the skills will therefore develop in the same manner and so transfer can occur. However, backhand shots in tennis and badminton are produced using different characteristic arm and wrist actions, and so negative transfer occurs easily. The movement patterns/subroutines of the skill appear to be the similar, but there are key differences. As a result, badminton and tennis shots should not be taught simultaneously. Negative transfer may also occur when an additional skill is introduced before the performer has grooved/overlearned the original skill.

Proactive transfer

This type of transfer can be positive or negative. Proactive transfer occurs when the learning and performance of a current skill has an effect (either positively or negatively) on a future skill that is yet to be learned/performed. For example, learning to serve in volleyball now will (positively) affect the learning and performance of the tennis serve in the future. It is important that young children learn and groove basic/fundamental skills, such as throwing and catching, as they will then be able to transfer these simple skills into more complex ones in the future. For example, successfully learning the overarm throw as a child enables positive transfer into several, more complex, sport-specific skills in a range of sports, such as fielding in cricket, serving in tennis, throwing a javelin, throwing from backstop to first base in rounders and the shoulder pass in netball.

Retroactive transfer

This type of transfer can also be positive or negative. Retroactive transfer occurs when the learning and performance of a skill has an effect, either positively or negatively, on a skill that has been learned and performed previously. For example, a hockey

Knowledge check 4

Define transfer of skills.

Identical elements theory The more the practice condition replicates the competitive situation, the more likely it is that positive transfer will occur.

Knowledge check 5

What is the difference between positive and negative transfer?

player decides to take up golf during the summer months. As they are learning and performing the golf drive, retroactive transfer to their hockey hit might occur. That is, learning the golf drive might have a negative effect when they go back to playing hockey, because their swing has become too high.

Bilateral transfer

This type of transfer describes when the learning and performing of a skill on one side of the body/limb allows it to be performed equally as well on the opposite side of the body/limb. For example, a performer who can dribble a basketball proficiently with the left hand might quickly become equally competent in dribbling with the right hand. Performers often learn to produce the skill on their preferred side/limb before attempting the skill on the other side/limb. There are obvious advantages in various sports of being able to effectively catch a ball with both hands or dribble a ball with both feet. Think about a snooker player who, by using bilateral transfer, can make successful shots with either arm. The angles they are able to manoeuvre the cue into are unrestricted because they are able to strike the ball effectively from their left or right side.

Optimising the effects of positive transfer

To optimise the effects of positive transfer the coach should:
- ensure the performer's first skill is grooved/overlearned
- highlight where positive transfer can take place, for example by pointing out the similarities in the subroutines
- give clear demonstrations of the skills that the performer can match
- ensure that the practice environments for both skills are similar, so it is clear that transfer can take place
- use varied practice methods
- make practice sessions as close to the game situation as possible (identical elements theory)
- give the performer praise, positive **reinforcement** and rewards when positive transfer takes place

Limiting the effects of negative transfer

To limit the effects of negative transfer the coach should:
- ensure that the first skill is grooved before the second skill is presented
- highlight where differences in the skill are, and therefore where negative transfer may take place
- ensure the performer understands all the components/subroutines of the skill
- not teach skills together that seem to lend themselves to transfer, but actually do not — for example, tennis and badminton shots

Knowledge check 6

Define proactive and retroactive transfer.

Reinforcement Praise or a reward offered by a coach when the performer is successful, to encourage them to repeat the correct actions/behaviours.

Summary

After studying this topic you should be able to:
- identify, describe and give examples of the five types of transfer — positive, negative, proactive, retroactive and bilateral
- give clear practical examples to illustrate each type of transfer, making sure that you clearly identify a specific skill rather than just the name of a sport
- explain how to optimise the effects of positive transfer, ensuring that you can offer at least four answers
- explain how to limit the effects of negative transfer, ensuring that you can offer at least four answers

Principles and theories of learning movement skills

Operant conditioning

This a connectionist/associationist theory. Psychologists such as Skinner suggest that learning occurs by creating a **link/association** between a **stimulus** and a **response**. This is known as the **S–R bond**. The coach allows the performer to use **trial-and-error learning** to work out the most effective way to perform the required skill. The coach may decide to **manipulate the environment** to improve the performer's success rate. The coach will offer positive reinforcement when the correct action is shown, so that the performer is motivated to repeat the movement and the S–R bond is strengthened. The performer's behaviour is therefore shaped/modified.

For example, the coach allows a cognitive tennis player to try out different ways of hitting the ball over the net using forehand strokes (trial and error). To increase the success rate the coach moves them closer to the net or may lower the height of the net (manipulating the environment). Each time the player is successful in getting the ball over the net the coach praises them (positive reinforcement). The player repeats the action and therefore their behaviour is shaped.

Thorndike's laws

Thorndike's three theoretical 'laws' are linked to operant conditioning. Thorndike suggested that these should be applied in order to create and strengthen an S–R bond.

The law of readiness
- An S–R bond can only be created and strengthened if the performer is mentally mature enough and physically able to cope with the demands of the task.
- If the performer is not mentally and physically able, the S–R bond will not be created.
- For example, the performer must be able to fully understand the components of the basketball lay-up and also be physically strong enough to perform the shot in order for the S–R bond to be created.

S–R bond The link/connection between a stimulus and a response.

Trial-and-error learning Occurs when the performer makes an attempt at a skill. If they are unsuccessful they will try an alternative method.

Manipulating the environment Involves changing the environment to make it easier for the performer to succeed.

The law of exercise

- The performer must practise/repeat the skill in order to strengthen the S–R bond.
- When the correct action is shown, reinforcement is required.
- If an action is not practised, this will weaken the S–R bond.
- For example, the performer must practise their lay-up repeatedly.

The law of effect

- When a correct action is shown, a 'satisfier' such as praise should be given to strengthen the S–R bond.
- When an incorrect action is shown, an 'annoyer' such as criticism should be given to weaken the S–R bond.
- For example, each time the correct lay-up action is shown by the performer, the coach should offer a satisfier such as praise. This reinforcement will encourage the performer to repeat the action and therefore strengthen the S–R bond. If the lay-up action is incorrect, the S–R bond needs to be weakened. This can be achieved by using an annoyer such as criticising the action. The performer is therefore unlikely to repeat this action in the future.

Reinforcement is a key aspect of both Skinner and Thorndike's theories. Reinforcement is the process in which the S–R bond is strengthened, and therefore increases the likelihood of the correct action/behaviour being repeated.

Positive reinforcement is used to strengthen the S–R bond. It is any form of approval offered to the performer when the successful action/behaviour is shown. This will increase their confidence and motivation and will encourage them to repeat the action. For example, a young dancer successfully spots their pirouettes. The dance teacher praises them and the dancer repeats the technique in the future.

Negative reinforcement is also used to strengthen the S–R bond. This is when, following a period of criticism regarding unsuccessful actions, the coach removes the negative criticism completely and says nothing once the successful action is demonstrated. For example, a coach is watching a swimmer performing front crawl and constantly criticises their low elbow position while walking along the poolside. As soon as the swimmer successfully demonstrates the required elbow position, the coach says nothing. The performer realises that, because they are not being criticised, the action must have been correct and therefore repeats the elbow action.

Punishment is used to weaken the S–R bond and to eliminate incorrect actions. It is any strategy used to stop the performer from repeating the incorrect action. This could be sin-binning a rugby player for an illegal high tackle, a penalty shot given to a netball goal shooter when she is contacted by the goalkeeper or even extra training given to a player who is persistently late for training sessions.

Exam tip

Do not confuse negative reinforcement with negative feedback. Remember, both positive reinforcement and negative reinforcement are offered when the correct actions/ behaviours are shown.

Knowledge check 7

Name Thorndike's laws.

Knowledge check 8

Define negative reinforcement.

Cognitive theory of learning

Gestalt psychologists, such as Köhler, suggest that individuals learn as they use their memories and previous knowledge to help them with the task in hand. 'Gestalt' refers to *wholeness* or entirety. This approach is also referred to as **insight learning**. Insight learning is a problem-solving approach where the performer uses their memory to help complete the task in hand.

Cognitive learning suggests that the whole is greater than the sum of its parts, and therefore the performer should learn by experiencing the whole task, because breaking it down into parts is ineffective. Whole learning ensures that the **kinaesthesis** and **flow** of the skill are maintained. For example, a performer should be allowed to attempt the full triple jump, rather than the individual parts.

Cognitive psychologists suggest that when learning using this method the performer is faced with **intervening variables**. This means that the performer goes through several mental processes, working out what to do and developing a greater understanding of the requirements by using their **perception**. This theory suggests that it is a better method than telling the performer what to do because it allows them to be creative and develop their own strategies and tactics. For example, a rugby player may work out which player is best to pass to in a pressure situation and so makes a judgement.

Finally, the performer will use their knowledge and **past experiences** of similar sporting situations to help with the task in hand. For example, a novice javelin thrower may remember throwing a ball overarm in cricket. They may also recall an experience of a long throw, where they turned sideways, and apply it to their javelin throw.

Bandura's theory of social/observational learning

Social learning and **observational learning** are interchangeable terms that both identify learning that happens by watching and copying the actions and behaviours of other people.

Bandura suggested that we learn by watching and replicating the actions of 'model' performers, who we respect and admire. These 'models' are known as 'significant others'. They may include our family members, coaches, teachers, peers or role models in the media.

Learners are more likely to copy:

- significant others
- models that have similar characteristics, for example age/gender
- actions that are performed successfully
- actions that are reinforced

> **Knowledge check 9**
>
> Why do Gestaltists say that part learning is ineffective?

> **Perception** Involves making a judgement based on the environmental stimuli you are presented with.

Bandura's model

The coach must ensure that the four key processes in the model (Figure 1) are used for learning to occur. The learner will then match the performance shown by the model.

MODEL DEMONSTRATION
- The coach requests that a performer demonstrates the required action to the learner
- For example, the coach asks a Year 11 pupil to demonstrate the high jump to a Year 7 pupil

↓

1 ATTENTION
- Coach ensures that the performer **concentrates** on the model
- Coach **highlights** key points of the demonstration. This is called cueing
- Model should be **attractive**, for example use a role model that the performer *wants* to watch
- For example, the Year 7 pupil looks up to the Year 11 pupil. They are an attractive role model. The coach points out the curved run-up, the position of the lead leg, the arms driving upwards and the bend in the back as the performer passes over the bar. The Year 7 student is fully attentive.

↓

2 RETENTION
- Coach ensures the performer remembers the demonstration
- Demonstration should be **repeated**
- A **clear mental image** should be created through visualisation or mental rehearsal
- For example, the Year 11 performer repeats the high jump several times and the coach asks the Year 7 pupil to go over the actions and key points in their mind

↓

3 MOTOR REPRODUCTION
- Performer must be **physically and mentally able** to copy the model demonstration
- For example, the Year 7 pupil must be able to understand the coaching points given to them and must be physically able to jump the height of the bar

↓

4 MOTIVATION
- The performer must have the **determination** to copy and learn the skill
- The coach could generate this by offering praise or rewards
- For example, the Year 7 pupil must want to learn to perform the high jump. The coach should praise the learner to motivate them to continue the learning process

↓

MATCHING PERFORMANCE
- The performer is able to produce the action that was demonstrated
- For example, through the four key processes described above, the Year 7 pupil now has the ability to produce the high jump

---

Figure 1 Bandura's model of observational learning

Cueing Occurs when the coach identifies the most important stimuli/subroutines and focuses the performer's attention on these.

Visualisation or **mental rehearsal** Going over the movement patterns of the skill in the mind without physically moving.

Exam tips

A common mistake that students make in relation to this model is describing motor reproduction as practising the skill that has been demonstrated. This is incorrect. This part of the model tells us that the performer must have the mental and physical capacity to produce the skill themselves. Do not fall into this trap.

Exam tips

If you are asked to explain the 'motivation' stage of the model, do not say that 'the performer must be motivated' because this is a repeat of the question and will not gain credit. Say that the performer must have the desire or drive to want to learn the skill.

Summary

After studying this topic you should be able to:

- explain how learning occurs, utilising the theories identified above — operant conditioning including Thorndike's laws, positive reinforcement, negative reinforcement and punishment, the cognitive theory of learning according to the Gestalt approach and Bandura's observational theory of learning
- apply your knowledge of each of the theories and illustrate them with clear practical examples of skills (not just sports)

Knowledge check 10

Identify the four key parts of Bandura's model.

Stages of learning

Fitts and Posner suggested that learners pass through three key stages of learning. As you would expect, all performers progress through the stages at different rates, and these vary from skill to skill. It is important that teachers and coaches have an understanding of the three stages. They can employ the most appropriate practice and transfer methods and assist in the learning process by using the most relevant feedback and guidance methods for the stage that the performer is in.

The cognitive stage

- A mental image is created.
- Demonstration is necessary to see what the skill looks like.
- Mental rehearsal is required.
- Many mistakes are made.
- Trial-and-error learning is a key feature.
- Movements are jerky and uncoordinated.
- All the performer's attention is on the production of the skill.
- Motor programmes are yet to be formed.

For example, a hockey player who is initially learning to dribble will be slow. Their movements will be jerky, and they will often lose the ball as a result of hitting it too hard. Their head will be down as they watch the ball intently. Because they do not yet know how it is supposed to feel, they rely on their coach for feedback. Their coach will give various demonstrations and the learner will watch and work out each subroutine. They should constantly mentally rehearse dribbling in this phase.

Feedback

- The performer is reliant on extrinsic feedback.
- Positive feedback maintains motivation.
- Some knowledge of results can be used.

The associative stage

- The performer must continue to practise to remain in and then progress from this stage.
- Some performers never progress beyond this stage.

Exam tip

Do not confuse the cognitive stage of learning with the cognitive *theory* of learning. This is a common mistake. Read the question carefully.

- Fewer mistakes are made.
- Smoother movements occur.
- The performer can begin to focus on the finer aspects of the skill/tactics.
- Motor programmes are developing.
- Demonstrations, positive feedback and mental rehearsal are still needed.

For example, a gymnast on a beam will have practised and mastered the basic skills and will now be able to execute more complex leaps and spins. They can now use intrinsic feedback, because they are beginning to become aware of how the movements should feel. They can now look up and forward rather than down at their feet.

Feedback
- Internal kinaesthesis begins to develop.
- Extrinsic feedback is still used to refine actions.
- The performer begins to use knowledge of performance.

The autonomous stage
- Movements are fluent and efficient.
- Skills are executed automatically without conscious thought.
- Motor programmes are fully formed.
- The performer can focus on fine detail, tactics and advanced strategies rather than the production of the skill.
- Practice and mental rehearsal are required to stay at this level.

For example, a basketball player will be able to dribble the ball fluently and consistently without having to look down at the ball. They are able to scan the court for passing options without concentrating on controlling the ball because it is being controlled automatically by the motor programme. They can correct any errors they make immediately, without assistance from the coach.

Feedback
- Internal kinaesthesis is used by the performer to correct their own mistakes.
- Extrinsic feedback is used infrequently to correct errors.
- Knowledge of performance is used readily.

Exam tip

Questions about the stages of learning often require you to identify the types of feedback that are used most effectively at each stage.

Summary

After studying this topic you should be able to:
- describe the characteristics of the three stages of learning — cognitive, associative and autonomous
- explain which types of feedback can be utilised at each stage — positive feedback, negative feedback, intrinsic feedback, extrinsic feedback, knowledge of results and knowledge of performance
- apply your knowledge of each of the theories and illustrate this with clear practical examples of skills (not just sports)

Guidance

Guidance is used by coaches to assist the performer when learning a new skill or developing more advanced, complex skills.

Types and uses of guidance

There are four types of guidance that a coach may decide to use. Before choosing to use one or more of the types of guidance, the coach will take into account the performer's stage of learning and motivation levels, as well as the skill being learned.

Visual guidance

Visual guidance allows the performer to see how to perform the skill. It is essential for cognitive performers. The demonstration must be accurate so that the performer sees how to perform the skill in the correct way. Examples include demonstrations, videos, coaching manuals or charts. For example, the coach shows the performer a video of how to perform a tumble turn in swimming correctly.

Advantages

- It shows the performer exactly what the skill should look like.
- It builds a clear mental image and highlights weaknesses in more advanced performers.

Disadvantages

- It can cause information overload, especially when a lot of information is presented at the same time.
- The demonstration must be accurate, or an incorrect movement pattern will be copied, so this relies on the ability of the coach being able to perform the skill accurately.

Verbal guidance

Verbal guidance involves giving the performer an explanation, and instructions on what to do and how to do it. For example, a swimming coach explains that the front crawl leg kick should come from the hip and not the knee. A basketball coach calls a timeout and instructs the players to adjust their tactics and run an X-cross set play.

Advantages

- It can be given immediately.
- It is useful for open skills and can be used effectively in conjunction with visual guidance.
- It can be used to give autonomous performers technical, strategic and tactical information.

Disadvantages

- There is a chance of information overload occurring if too many instructions are given together, so the performer may lose concentration.
- Cognitive performers may not understand the technical terms used by their coach.
- It relies on the coach being able to explain what is required in a clear, concise and accurate way.

Knowledge check 11

What are the advantages and disadvantages of verbal guidance?

Manual guidance

Manual guidance is the use of physical support, or when a coach forces a response from the performer. For example, a swimming coach holds a beginner swimmer up in the water to keep them afloat. A golf coach stands behind the performer and, with their hands on top, guides the performer through the drive swing.

Advantages

- It is effective for cognitive performers.
- It can be used for dangerous tasks because it improves safety during performance, while also reducing fear/anxiety.
- It allows the performer to build their confidence.
- Because the whole skill can be attempted, kinaesthesis can be developed.

Disadvantages

- The performer may become reliant on it and may also become demotivated.
- Incorrect kinaesthesis can be developed and, as a result, bad habits might form.
- The physical contact or close proximity of the coach may make the performer feel uncomfortable and/or could be misconstrued.

Mechanical guidance

Mechanical guidance is the use of equipment to aid and shape movement — for example, using a swimming float/armband for safety. A trampoline coach uses a rig and harness to teach the front somersault for the first time. The performer is then able to experience the feeling of the whole movement immediately and safely.

Advantages

- It is effective for cognitive performers.
- It can be used for dangerous tasks because it improves safety during performance, while also reducing fear/anxiety.
- It allows the performer to build their confidence.
- Because the whole skill can be attempted, kinaesthesis can be developed.

Disadvantages

- The performer may become reliant on it and may also become demotivated.
- Incorrect kinaesthesis can be developed and, as a result, bad habits might form.

Exam tip

You may be asked to 'critically evaluate' the types of guidance. This means that you must give advantages and disadvantages and relate the types of guidance to practical examples.

Summary

After studying this topic you should be able to:

- describe each method of guidance — visual, verbal, manual and mechanical
- apply your knowledge by stating how each type of guidance can be used to promote the learning and development of specific skills
- describe the advantages and disadvantages of each type of guidance

Feedback

Feedback is any information received about a performance either during or after the performance. Feedback is important because it tells the performer what to do to correct errors and it prevents any incorrect actions reoccurring, thus preventing bad habits from developing. It can also reinforce correct actions so that they are repeated. Feedback will also improve the performer's confidence and motivation.

Feedback should be:

- specific to the task in hand
- given in brief, manageable chunks to aid understanding
- compared with previous attempts at the skill, to highlight progression
- given immediately
- linked to the performer's personal goals

Types and uses of feedback

Intrinsic feedback

Intrinsic feedback is information received from within, using kinaesthesis. It is used to 'feel' if the action was correct or not. It can be positive or negative.

Advantages

- The performer can detect and correct their own errors.
- It is used immediately, as the movement is happening.

Disadvantages

- Cognitive performers cannot use this type of feedback.

Extrinsic feedback

Extrinsic feedback is information received from an outside source. It can be positive or negative.

Advantages

- Correct actions are reinforced.
- Errors are corrected.

Disadvantages

- The information given must be accurate or the performer will not develop.
- Kinaesthesis is not promoted using this method.
- Performers may become reliant on it.

Positive feedback

Positive feedback involves information about what was *correct*, so that the action/technique will be repeated in the future.

Advantages

- Motivation and confidence are increased.
- S–R bonds can be created and strengthened.

Disadvantages

- If it is overused it loses its impact.

- Some performers dislike receiving praise, especially in a public forum. It may therefore have the opposite of the desired effect.

Negative feedback

Negative feedback is information about incorrect actions, so that errors are corrected.

Advantages

- The performer knows what to do to improve.
- Some performers also use negative feedback as a motivational tool.

Disadvantages

- If used excessively it can demotivate the performer.
- It should be used carefully with cognitive performers.
- It can result in the performer withdrawing completely from participation.

Knowledge of results

Knowledge of results is information about whether or not the skill/action was successful.

Advantages

- It can be used by cognitive performers.
- It is motivational.

Disadvantages

- It does not explain why the action was a success or failure.
- It is ineffective for autonomous performers.
- It can also be demotivating if the performer is repeatedly unsuccessful.

Knowledge of performance

Knowledge of performance is information about why the skill/action was successful/unsuccessful. It can be positive or negative, internal or external.

Advantages

- It includes technical information about the performance.
- It can be used by autonomous performers.
- It allows the performer to utilise their kinaesthesis.

Disadvantages

- Cognitive performers may not understand the technical information and may become overloaded.
- It can be demotivating if the performer is repeatedly unsuccessful.

Knowledge check 12

Identify the six types of feedback.

Knowledge check 13

Why do coaches give feedback?

Summary

After studying this topic you should be able to:
- describe each type of feedback — positive feedback, negative feedback, intrinsic feedback, extrinsic feedback, knowledge of results and knowledge of performance
- apply your knowledge by stating how each type of feedback can be used to promote the learning and development of specific skills
- describe the advantages and disadvantages of each type of feedback, making sure you give a balance of positives and negatives

Memory models

Atkinson and Shiffren's multi-store memory model

Three components make up the multi-store model (Figure 2). You need to understand the features and functions of each.

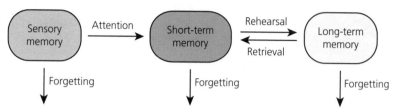

Figure 2 Atkinson and Shiffren's multi-store memory model

1 Short-term sensory store/sensory memory

- All the information, whether relevant or irrelevant, is held temporarily for approximately 0.25–1 second.
- It is a large store of limitless capacity.
- **Selective attention** is operational. The relevant stimuli are attended to while the irrelevant are disregarded. For example, a tennis player will focus on the ball when serving and disregard the crowd. This is important because it:
  - aids concentration
  - improves reaction time
  - filters out any distractions
  - controls arousal levels
  - reduces the chance of information overload in the short-term memory (STM)

2 Short-term memory

- This is known as the 'working memory' or workspace.
- It has a limited storage space of 7 ± 2 items.
- Capacity can be increased through **chunking**.
- Information is stored for up to 30 seconds, but this can be increased through practice.
- It is responsible for executing the motor programme.
- Important information is encoded and passed to the long-term memory (LTM).
- Information that is not considered important is lost.

3 Long-term memory

- Information enters the LTM through practice or rehearsal.
- Information can be stored permanently.
- Important information is encoded, while unimportant information is lost.
- It has unlimited capacity, with a 'lifetime' of memories.
- Motor programmes for all skills are stored as a result of lengthy practice.
- The STM retrieves motor programmes from the LTM to use.

Selective attention
The filtering of information. Relevant information is retained and attended to while irrelevant information is disregarded to increase the capacity of the short-term memory.

Chunking is when several stimuli or bits of information are grouped together and remembered as one piece of information to increase the capacity of the short-term memory.

Craik and Lockhart's levels of processing model

Craik and Lockhart's approach opposes the view that there are a number of memory stores. Their focus is on what we do with the information, rather than how it is stored. According to this model, how deeply we consider and process information will determine how long the memory trace will last.

If the information is understood by the performer and is meaningful to them — that is, it can be related to memories of past experiences — then it is more likely to be remembered. The meaning of the information is more relevant than how much repetition the performer undertakes.

For example, when learning the overarm serve in volleyball, the coach explains to the performer that the fundamental movement patterns are the same as the tennis serve. The performer considers and understands this and their memories of performing the tennis serve make it meaningful to them.

Summary

After studying this topic you should be able to:
- describe Atkinson and Shiffren's multi-store model of memory, including the short-term sensory store/sensory memory, short-term memory and long-term memory
- describe selective attention and how it is used to enable performers to focus their attention on the relevant stimuli while ignoring the irrelevant items in the environment
- describe Craik and Lockhart's levels of processing model .
- apply your knowledge of both models to illustrate the learning and performance of physical activity skills

■ Sports psychology

By studying sports psychology, you will develop knowledge and understanding of the individual psychological differences that can affect performers when participating in physical activity and sport. You will also understand how group/team dynamics can affect participation.

You will understand how important goal setting and the use of appropriate attributions are in motivating performers. You will also develop knowledge and understanding of the role of self-confidence and self-efficacy in sport, the effects of leadership in sport, and how stress management strategies can optimise performance.

Individual differences

Personality

Personality is what makes an individual unique. It is their qualities, character and behaviours that make them different from other people.

Psychologists dispute how personality is developed. Some believe that personality is mostly natural, while others believe that it is mostly learnt. This gives rise to the **nature versus nurture debate**.

Nature versus nurture debate The dispute between trait and social learning theories of personality, aggression and leadership

Theories of personality

Trait theory

The trait theory of personality suggests that a performer is born with their personality, it is determined genetically, and that these characteristics will most likely be shown in all situations. Therefore, behaviour can be predicted. Trait psychologists suggest that personality is stable and enduring; in other words, your personality does not change and is permanent. For example, a netballer who is calm and controlled will always show these characteristics even when playing against an opponent who is continually contacting her. Her coach would be confident that the player would not lash out, despite the contact. This approach does not consider any effects that environmental learning may have on the performer, or that they may consciously decide to structure their own personality. This is the basis of the nature (trait) versus nurture (social learning) debate.

Trait theorists suggest that an individual's personality lies on two continua, between extroversion/introversion and stability/neurosis (Table 1).

Table 1 Personality traits

Extroversion/introversion		Stability/neurosis	
Extroverts	**Introverts**	**Stable**	**Neurotic**
Like social situations Are outgoing Like performing with an audience Become bored easily because the **RAS** is not easily stimulated	Dislike social situations Are reserved/shy Dislike performing in front of an audience Are easily over-aroused because the RAS is easily stimulated	Reliable Consistent Calm	Unpredictable Restless Volatile

RAS The reticular activating system — the part of the brain that regulates arousal.

The four quadrants can be used to describe individuals' personalities. For example, a stable extrovert would be even-tempered and outgoing, while a stable introvert would be consistent and reserved. A neurotic extrovert would be ill-tempered and lively, while a neurotic introvert would be unpredictable and shy.

Type A and type B personalities

This is also a trait theory, which suggests that performers fall into one of two types of personality:

Type A personalities:
■ are prone to experiencing high stress/arousal levels
■ are very competitive
■ are intolerant of others
■ need to be in control of the task — they find it hard to delegate
■ tend to work fast

Type B personalities:
■ are likely to have low stress/arousal levels
■ are not concerned with competition
■ tend to be patient
■ do not need to be in control of the task — can delegate tasks
■ work slowly

Social learning theory

This theory suggests that personality is not innate but is learned from our experiences. It changes according to the situation, so behaviour cannot be predicted. We observe and copy the personality of significant others such as parents, peers, coaches and role models in the media. **Socialisation** also plays an important part. If the personality/behaviour is deemed successful or is praised by a coach, it is highly likely that the performer will imitate that personality/behaviour. For example, your tennis coach constantly praises your teammate for showing determination and controlled emotions. You decide to copy their behaviour in order to gain the same reinforcement.

A performer is more likely to copy the behaviour/personality of those who share similar characteristics, such as gender, age and ability level, as well as those who are significant to them.

Interactionist theory

This theory states that personality is made up of both your traits and the influence of what you have learned from your environmental experiences. It accepts that parts of both the trait and social learning approaches are relevant, so combines them. The equation to describe this is:

$$B = f(P \times E)$$

Behaviour B is a function (f) of an individual's personality traits (P) and the environment (E). This theory suggests that a performer will adapt to the situation they find themselves in, even behaving differently from how they normally would. For example, a generally introverted rhythmic gymnast adapts and displays more extroverted characteristics during a competition in order to appeal to the judges.

Knowledge check 14

What is the difference between an extrovert and introvert?

Socialisation Adopting the norms that surround you.

Exam tip

If the question asks you about the nature versus nurture debate, ensure that you explain both trait theory and social learning theory. To really boost your marks, conclude with a statement about the interactionist perspective.

Exam tip

Trait, social learning and interactionist theories feature in personality, aggression and leadership. Tailor practical examples to the specific area of the specification.

Attitudes

An attitude is a strongly held opinion that predisposes an individual to think, feel and act, either positively or negatively, towards an attitude object. Attitudes are subjective.

An **attitude object** is the focus of the individual's attitude. This can be other people, ideas/concepts, geographical places, events and specific objects/items.

Factors affecting attitude formation

Attitudes can be positive or negative. They are developed through experiences rather than being innate, and often begin to form at an early age. Attitudes are stable and enduring — that is, once one is formed, it will be long-lasting and can be difficult to change.

Attitude formation can occur via the following:

- **Social learning** — attitudes can form as individuals observe and imitate the attitudes of people who are significant to them. Significant others can be family members, peers, teachers/coaches and role models in the media. If your parents/ friends have a positive attitude towards sport/physical activity, it is likely that you will copy them, especially if you are reinforced or praised for doing so by a coach. High-profile role models in the media often display positive attitudes and, as we regard them highly, we are likely to adopt their positive attitude. The opposite is also true, because negative attitudes can be formed if those around you demonstrate negativity.
- **Socialisation** — when an individual wishes to fit in with the cultural norms surrounding them, they adopt the values and attitudes of those they associate with. If it is the norm for your friendship group or family to participate in sport regularly, and they have positive attitudes towards physical activity, then you will conform in order to fit in. For example, they might all enjoy badminton and play for a team, or attend the gym on a regular basis. You then do the same, often because you do not want to feel left out.
- **Past experiences** — your direct experiences undoubtedly contribute to attitude formation. If you have had positive experiences or experienced success, such as enjoying playing sport, winning matches or titles, this can generate a positive attitude and increase motivation. Likewise, negative past experiences, such as failure or injury, can contribute to the formation of negative attitudes.
- **Reinforcement** — as explained by **operant conditioning**, reinforcement can be used to ensure that correct behaviours, or in this case attitudes, are repeated. If a coach praises your positive attitude towards pre-season training, this strengthens your beliefs and behaviours. The opposite is also true — if negative attitudes towards sport are reinforced, a negative attitude can be formed.

Components of attitudes

The **triadic model** suggests that an attitude is made up of three components:

- **Cognitive** — this component describes an individual's beliefs and thoughts. For example, I believe that attending CrossFit classes is good for my physical and mental health.
- **Affective** — this component describes an individual's emotions and feelings. For example, I enjoy attending CrossFit classes and feel energised afterwards.
- **Behavioural** — this component describes an individual's actions/responses. For example, I participate in CrossFit classes five times each week.

Knowledge check 15

What are the three components of an attitude?

Knowledge check 16

How are attitudes formed?

Exam tip

Questions may ask you to explain the triadic model. Clearly explain all components. Students often confuse the components and, as a result, do not gain credit.

Methods of attitude change

Cognitive dissonance

When an individual's attitude components all match, whether positively or negatively, they are in a state of cognitive consonance. Their beliefs, feelings and actions are in harmony and the individual's attitude will remain steady. One way to change an attitude is to create **cognitive dissonance** (Table 2). Dissonance is caused by generating unease within the individual. This unease is created by changing one of more of the negative attitude components into a positive, thus causing the individual to question their attitude and increase their motivation to change.

Table 2 Ways to create cognitive dissonance by destabilising each attitude component

Negative attitude		Change by
Cognitive	I think that going to the gym is a waste of time	Educating them — provide them with credible information that challenges their attitude; preferably, this should be given by a significant other Highlight to them that attending the gym can improve physical and mental health
Affective	I hate going to the gym	Ensuring a positive, varied experience Make it fun/enjoyable Ensure success, so their confidence and motivation increases
Behavioural	I do not go to the gym	Using persuasive communication, preferably by a specialist, to encourage them to attend a session at the gym Praise/reinforce them

Persuasive communication

Persuasive communication is when an individual/group of people encourages you to take on board their point of view, resulting in a change in attitude. To increase the likelihood of persuasive communication being effective:

- the person trying to persuade should have high status/be significant to the performer, and also have strong communication skills
- the persuader should have credibility, that is, be knowledgeable/proficient/expert
- the message should be clear, correct and explicit
- the person who is listening to the message must understand the information and ultimately be open to change
- peers/other significant people may also be used to support the persuader when giving the message in order to strengthen their case

Motivation

Motivation is a person's desire to succeed. It is an individual's drive that inspires them to perform in sport. This can happen in two ways.

Extrinsic motivation

Extrinsic motivation is the drive you receive from an outside source. There are two types of extrinsic motivation — **tangible** and **intangible**.

Tangible rewards are physical items such as money, trophies, medals and certificates. For example, a swimmer receives a certificate for completing the Stage 1 Award.

Knowledge check 17

What is cognitive dissonance?

Intangible rewards are non-physical, and include praise from the coach or supportive chants from the crowd. For example, the coach shouts 'well done' when the triathlete transitions quickly and effectively from the bike to run stage.

Extrinsic rewards attract performers to the sport in the first instance. This approach is therefore useful for cognitive performers. It also raises their confidence. However, performers may become reliant on the coach or other people. If tangible and/or intangible motivation are used excessively, they can lose their impact and therefore should be offered appropriately.

Intrinsic motivation

Intrinsic motivation is the drive that comes from within the performer. The individual participates for the 'love' of the sport and/or the pride of achieving their own goals. This type of motivation is essential for the performer if they are to maintain participation. If a coach generates this in their performers, it can be much more effective than extrinsic motivation. Individuals will have a greater level of task persistence if they are intrinsically motivated.

Arousal

Arousal is the level of somatic or cognitive stimulation that gets us ready to perform. **Somatic** refers to the body — it is physiological. **Cognitive** refers to the mind — it is psychological.

Drive theory

Drive theory suggests that as arousal increases then so does performance quality — linearly (Figure 3). In other words, the more drive the performer has, the better their performance will be. This results in a proportionally increased performance.

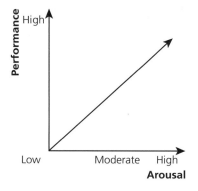

Figure 3 Drive theory

This theory suggests that at high arousal the performer feels the pressure and therefore reverts to using their **dominant response**. This is a well-learned skill that the performer will use when under competitive pressure.

If the performer is in the autonomous phase of learning, their dominant response is likely to be performed correctly. However, cognitive performers are not able to cope with the high levels of arousal and therefore their dominant response is likely to be performed incorrectly. The equation to describe this is:

$$P = f(D \times H)$$

where performance (P) is a function of drive (D) multiplied by habit (H).

Inverted-U theory

The inverted-U theory suggests that as arousal level increases so does performance quality, up to an optimum point (moderate arousal). Beyond this point, performance quality decreases as a result of over-arousal. Both under-arousal and over-arousal result in lower performance quality. This optimum point varies according to the performer, their personality type and the skill being performed (Figure 4).

Knowledge check 20

According to the inverted-U theory, at what level of arousal do performers generally achieve optimum performance?

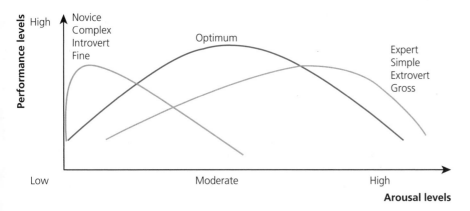

Figure 4 How the task, the performer and their personality can affect the level of arousal required for optimal performance

In Figure 4 the green curve shows where optimum performance occurs at lower levels of arousal. This is characteristic of:

- **cognitive performers**, because they are inexperienced and unable to deal with high levels of arousal
- **fine skills** that require a high level of precision and control — to maintain accuracy, low levels of arousal produce more effective results
- **complex skills**, which require several decisions to be made and so are more effective at low levels of arousal
- **introverts**, who have an easily stimulated reticular activating system (RAS, see page 28) and therefore perform better at low levels of arousal

The blue curve shows where optimum performance occurs at higher levels of arousal. This is characteristic of:

- **autonomous performers**, who are experienced and therefore able to perform successfully with increased arousal levels
- **gross skills**, which do not require precision and control and so can be performed at high levels of arousal
- **simple skills**, which require few decisions to be made and so are more effective at high arousal levels
- **extroverts**, who experience low stimulation of the RAS, meaning they strive for 'exciting' situations, and are thus able to perform when arousal levels are high

Catastrophe theory

This accounts for the sudden drop seen in performance, once the moderate level of arousal has been exceeded (Figure 5). Catastrophe theory is multidimensional, considering the effects of both cognitive (psychological) and somatic (physiological) anxiety. It suggests that as arousal increases so does performance quality up to an optimum point at moderate arousal, as shown by the inverted-U theory. There is then a dramatic decrease in performance as a result of high cognitive anxiety combined with high somatic anxiety. The body and the mind have become over-aroused, causing an immediate decline in performance — the catastrophe.

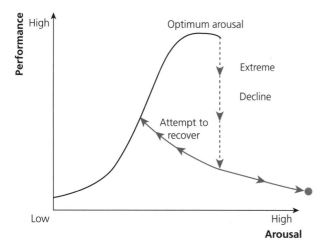

Figure 5 Catastrophe theory

The effects of the catastrophe can be reversed by performing relaxation techniques, such as deep breathing exercises or progressive muscular relaxation.

Anxiety

Anxiety is a negative emotion. It causes the performer to experience worry, fear and apprehension. In sport, anxiety can be felt for a variety of reasons. For example:

- when the task is important, such as playing in a cup final
- if the performer is new to the sport, such as a cognitive judo player attempting to receive her first belt
- if a lot of spectators are present

There are two types of anxiety:

- **Trait anxiety** is a stable and enduring emotion experienced by the performer. The performer is predisposed to feelings of worry and fear. Performers with trait anxiety experience nervousness in all competitions, regardless of the type or importance of event — for example, worrying and sweating before every match.
- **State anxiety** is a temporary and specific emotion that is only experienced by the performer in certain competitions/particular aspects of the event. Performers with state anxiety experience apprehension and fear relating to some parts of their performance, but not others. For example, the football player only thinks irrational thoughts when taking a penalty. A squash player experiences high blood pressure during finals only.

As a result of trait and/or state anxiety, the performer may experience changes in their body and/or mental state.

Knowledge check 21

What causes the 'catastrophe', according to catastrophe theory?

- **Cognitive anxiety** describes the psychological symptoms of anxiety, such as worrying, irrational thoughts and confusion. Learned helplessness may occur (page 45).
- **Somatic anxiety** refers to physiological symptoms, such as increase in heart rate, blood pressure, sweating and muscle tension.

Zone of optimal functioning

The zone is a positive mental state that performers normally only experience once/twice in their entire sporting career, when everything is 'perfect'. Characteristics of the zone include:

- feeling completely calm
- having complete control — being fully concentrated on the task
- performing on 'autopilot' — some performers have no memory of it
- feeling completely confident that success is inevitable
- performing with fluidity — smoothly and efficiently

Hanin suggested that optimum performance is reached during a band or zone, and not at a precise point as described by the inverted-U theory. In Figure 6, performer A enters the zone, achieving best performance at low levels of arousal; performer B is in the zone at moderate levels of arousal; and performer C enters the zone at high levels of arousal.

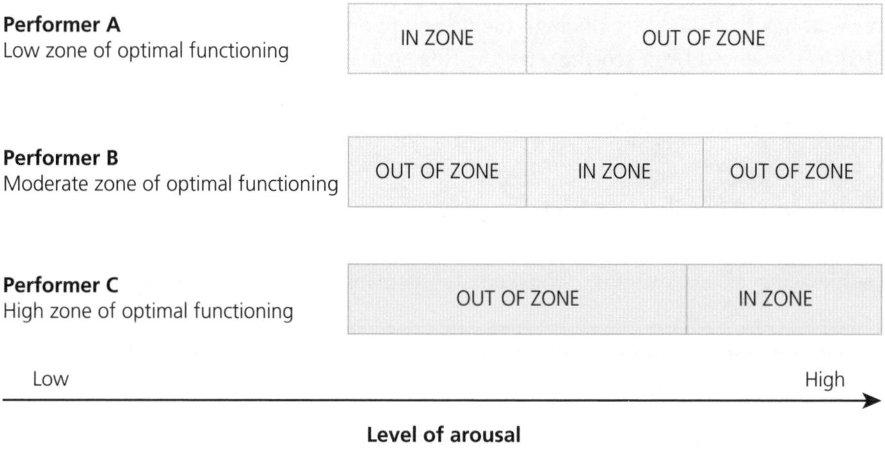

Performer A
Low zone of optimal functioning

IN ZONE	OUT OF ZONE

Performer B
Moderate zone of optimal functioning

OUT OF ZONE	IN ZONE	OUT OF ZONE

Performer C
High zone of optimal functioning

OUT OF ZONE	IN ZONE

Low ——————————————→ High

Level of arousal

Figure 6 The zone of optimal functioning

Aggression

Aggression is:

- the intent to harm
- outside the rules
- reactive
- out of control
- deliberate/hostile

For example, in rugby league, the tackled player gets off the ground to play the ball. As he does this, he angrily punches the tackler, which is outside the rules.

Theories of aggression

Instinct theory

According to this theory:

- We have a natural trait or predisposition to be aggressive.
- This trait is genetic — we are born with a natural tendency to defend ourselves/our territory.
- Aggression inevitably builds up.
- With enough provocation, we will respond aggressively.
- Once the aggressive act is complete, we experience catharsis.

For example, a wicketkeeper continually sledges a batsman in cricket. Eventually the batsman retaliates as a result of the continual provocation, and pushes the wicketkeeper.

Social learning theory

This theory opposes the trait approach and is based on the work of Bandura. It suggests that individuals learn how to behave aggressively by watching and copying **significant others**. If the aggression of these significant others is reinforced and/or is successful, their actions are more likely to be copied. Socialisation (see page 29) also plays an important part because individuals wish to fit in with the social norms. Aggression is more likely to be copied if the model shares similar characteristics with the performer, such as age, gender and skill level.

For example, a young rugby player watches their idol illegally high tackle an opponent. The crowd cheers and the opponent is prevented from scoring a try. As this aggressive act is performed by a significant other, and their aggressive act is reinforced and successful, the young player copies this behaviour in their next match.

Frustration–aggression hypothesis

This theory states that experiencing frustration will always lead to aggressive behaviour. It works as follows:

- The performer has a drive to achieve a goal. For example, a basketballer is dribbling towards the basket to score.
- Their goal is blocked. For example, the defender fouls the player.
- The player experiences frustration, which leads inevitably to aggression. For example, the player hits out at the defender.
- If the aggression is successfully released and avoids punishment, it leads to catharsis. For example, the player then feels better and continues to play.
- Alternatively, if the aggressive act is punished, this will lead to further frustration and therefore more aggression. For example, the official calls a foul and turns the ball over. The player feels even more frustrated and commits an illegal tackle on the opposition.

Aggressive cue hypothesis

This theory suggests that when a goal is blocked, the performer is in a state of 'readiness' for an aggressive act to occur. However, aggression is not inevitable.

- Once the performer's arousal levels are increased, this leads to frustration.
- The aggressive act is more likely to occur if learned cues/triggers are present.
- If these cues/triggers are not present, the aggressive act becomes less likely.

> **Knowledge check 23**
>
> What is catharsis?

> **Exam tip**
>
> A common mistake is to confuse theories of aggression with *causes* of aggression. Read the question carefully.

For example, potentially aggressive objects such as bats/clubs/sticks, or contact sports such as rugby/ice hockey, are more likely to produce aggressive responses. So, if an ice hockey player is tackled illegally, they are more likely to strike their opponent than a swimmer who is kicked underwater by their opponent in the next lane. A footballer who has been praised by their coach for aggressive, dangerous tackles may learn that this is a positive behaviour. The coach's shouts from the sideline may then act as a cue in future matches to be aggressive.

Social facilitation

Performers react differently to performing when other people are present. The 'others' may/may not be watching or competing directly against the performer, but simply by being in the same environment as other people, their performance can be affected.

Some enjoy performing with other people present and use the opportunity to demonstrate their prowess. This creates a positive effect and, as a result, their performance improves. This is **social facilitation**. However, some people dislike performing with an audience, and their performance worsens when in the same environment as others. Even if the 'others' are not directly observing or making judgements on the performer, a negative effect is felt. This is **social inhibition**.

Zajonc suggested that four types of 'others' may be present during a performance (Figure 7).

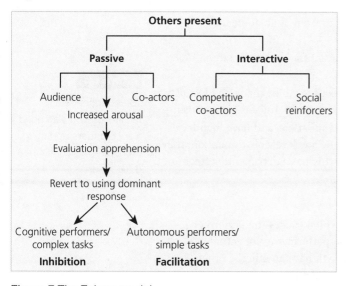

Figure 7 The Zajonc model

Passive others do not interact with the performer, but by being present they can have an effect:

- Audience — they do not speak but just watch. For example, the silent observers during a tee-off in golf/a scout turning up unannounced. Their presence makes you feel anxious and can affect your performance.
- Co-actors — they perform the same task at the same time but are not competing against you. For example, seeing another cyclist in front of you makes you speed up to overtake them. You win nothing by doing so, but their presence made you cycle faster.

Interactive others communicate directly with the performer:

- Competitive co-actors — the opposition. For example, other swimmers in a race who are in direct opposition to you.
- Social reinforcers/supporters — the coach/crowd. For example, the spectators at a football match might cheer or shout abuse at you.

When others are present, the main effect is that the performer experiences an increase in arousal. This causes the performer to revert to using their dominant response. They may also experience evaluation apprehension.

Social facilitation is likely to occur when:

- the performer is autonomous — they are used to performing in front of an audience
- performing a **gross** skill — where large muscle group movements do not require precision/accuracy
- performing a **simple** skill — requiring limited decision-making/information processing
- the performer is an **extrovert** — they seek social situations and have low levels of natural arousal, meaning their RAS is activated only by high levels of stimulation; they see the presence of the audience as an opportunity to 'show off', and rise to the challenge

Social inhibition is likely to occur when:

- the performer is cognitive — they find performing in front of an audience intimidating
- performing a **fine** skill — precision and accuracy are difficult to maintain at high arousal
- performing a **complex** skill — requiring several decisions to be made and lots of information processing, which may not be performed successfully at high arousal
- the performer is an **introvert** — they dislike social situations and have high levels of natural arousal, meaning their RAS is activated by low levels of stimulation; they find performing in front of others demanding, and this has a detrimental effect on their performance

Evaluation apprehension

Evaluation apprehension is the fear of being judged, which causes the performer to revert back to their dominant response. Even if the performer is not actually being judged, if they *perceive* that they are, then this will have an effect on their performance. Other factors can cause evaluation apprehension:

- If the audience is knowledgeable, then the performer will feel more nervous, for example if a scout is watching.
- If significant others such as parents/peers are present.
- If the audience is supportive/abusive, performance will be facilitated/inhibited.
- If the performer naturally has high trait anxiety, they will be inhibited by an audience.
- If they have low self-efficacy and do not believe in their ability, they will be inhibited.
- The proximity and size of the audience — a large audience that is close to the playing area can have a greater positive or negative effect.

> **Exam tip**
>
> To understand social facilitation you also need a solid understanding of arousal — particularly drive theory.

> **Knowledge check 26**
>
> What is evaluation apprehension?

Strategies to eliminate the effects of social inhibition

There are various strategies that performers and coaches can use to combat the negative effects experienced when an audience is present. These include:

- **familiarisation** training — allowing an audience to watch you training/playing crowd noises during training
- increasing **self-efficacy** (see Bandura's model, page 48)
- **practising** skills until they are grooved/overlearned
- **selective attention** — blocking out the crowd and concentrating on the relevant stimuli, such as the ball/opposition
- **mental rehearsal** — going over the performance in your mind maintains focus and lowers arousal levels
- **imagery**
- positive **self-talk**
- blocking out negative thoughts

In addition, the coach could:

- decrease the importance of the task
- support the performer by offering encouragement, positive reinforcement and praise

Summary

After studying this topic you should be able to:

Personality

- give a clear definition of personality
- explain how personality is developed, with reference to trait theory, social learning theory and interactionist theory
- use practical examples to illustrate each theory, ensuring that they are clearly linked to personality and not to learning sporting skills

Attitudes

- clearly define attitudes
- explain the factors affecting the formation of attitudes, including social learning theory, socialisation, past experiences and reinforcement
- describe the three components of an attitude — cognitive, affective and behavioural
- explain the methods used to change attitudes, including persuasive communication and cognitive dissonance
- illustrate each of the above with clear, practical examples

Motivation

- define intrinsic and extrinsic motivation, and illustrate these with practical examples
- explain how both methods can be used by performers at each stage of learning — cognitive, associative and autonomous
- explain the positive and negative effects of intrinsic motivation and extrinsic motivation on the performer

Arousal

- describe each of the three theories of arousal — drive theory, inverted-U theory and catastrophe theory
- use practical examples to illustrate each of the three theories of arousal

Anxiety
- explain and give examples of the four types of anxiety — state, trait, cognitive and somatic
- describe what it is like to be 'in the zone' of optimal functioning

Aggression
- give a clear definition of aggression
- give practical examples of aggressive acts in sport
- explain the four theories of aggression: instinct theory, the frustration/aggression hypothesis, the aggressive cue hypothesis and social learning theory
- give practical examples to illustrate each of the four theories of aggression

Social facilitation
- define social facilitation and social inhibition
- explain the effects of the audience on personality types (introverts and extroverts), performers (beginners/cognitive performers and experts/ autonomous performers) and skills (simple/complex skills and gross/fine skills)
- define and explain evaluation apprehension
- describe strategies to minimise social inhibition

Group and team dynamics in sport

Group and team dynamics refers to the study of groups and group members, and how they operate. A group is two or more people who:

- **interact** with each other — communicate through recognised channels
- share a **common goal** — they have the same aim
- have **mutual awareness** — they influence and depend on each other
- have a collective identity

Tuckman suggested that in order to become a group, rather than a collection of individuals, members go through four key stages: forming, storming, norming and performing (Table 3).

Knowledge check 27

What are the characteristics of a group?

Knowledge check 28

What are the four stages of group development according to Tuckman?

Table 3 Forming, storming, norming and performing

Forming	Storming	Norming	Performing
■ Working out if they belong with the group ■ Learning about other members/coaches ■ Developing social relationships ■ Figuring out the goal/ roles ■ Reliant on coach to bring the group closer ■ For example, during your first training sessions you decide that you want to be part of the hockey team because they seem to share your passion to win; you begin to socialise with other team members	■ Infighting and conflict occur ■ Cliques form ■ Teams often fold ■ Confrontation with the leaders occurs ■ Members actively challenge for their role/ position ■ Self-preservation is important ■ For example, both you and another netball team member wish to be the goalkeeper, which causes rivalry between you; you may also believe that the captain is not a strong enough leader and that you could do a better job	■ Conflicts are resolved ■ Group cohesion develops as members become unified/consensus is reached ■ Norms are set ■ Members cooperate to achieve potential ■ Motivation and success levels rise ■ Increased respect for leader and their style ■ For example, you decide that your teammate is an effective goalkeeper and that you can use your skills in an outfield position, giving the team an excellent defence; you respect the captain and are aware of their qualities	■ Group is stabilised ■ Fully concentrated on group succeeding ■ Motivation and enjoyment are high ■ Respect for other members and leaders is high ■ Goal and vision clear to all ■ Disagreements are resolved internally without affecting rest of the team negatively ■ For example, your team plays regularly and members praise each other for the team's success, which they find is increasing as they are now a unit

Steiner's model

Steiner suggested the following model, which explains why, when a coach brings together a collection of 'star' performers, they are not automatically successful. Steiner suggested that the greatest success is achieved by the most cohesive team, not by the team that has the best individuals.

actual productivity = potential productivity – losses due to faulty processes

Actual productivity is the team's level of achievement on a specific task, for example reaching the semi-final of a cup competition.

Potential productivity is the team's best possible level of achievement when it is cohesive, taking into consideration the ability of the players and resources available to them. For example, the team could have won the cup competition because they had the ability and track record.

Losses due to faulty processes are the coordination/cooperation and motivation problems the team faces. These reduce the level of cohesion and therefore lower their level of achievement — for example, some team members lacked the motivation to attend training, so they could not fully practice set plays. This had a negative impact on the coordination of the team, causing set plays to break down in the semi-final.

Steiner suggested that teams face many problems that affect their productivity, including:

- coordination problems — team members failing to communicate properly with each other, resulting in poor timing/set plays breaking down
- lack of understanding of their roles in the team
- lack of understanding of tactics or strategies set by the coach
- motivation losses, such as team members withdrawing effort when training and/or competing
- the Ringelmann effect
- social loafing

> **Knowledge check 29**
>
> State the equation that describes Steiner's model of productivity.

The Ringelmann effect and social loafing

The Ringelmann effect and **social loafing** are both faulty processes that have a detrimental effect on the cohesiveness and attainment of a team. Long-term effects include performers withdrawing from and/or avoiding sporting activity altogether, thus leading a sedentary lifestyle, with a detrimental effect on their health.

The Ringelmann effect was suggested after a 'tug-of-war' experiment showed that eight participants failed to pull eight times as hard as a single participant. Ringelmann's study found that as the number of people in the group increased, the level of performance of individuals in the group decreased. An example is a rugby union player performing much better when playing in a seven-a-side tournament than when playing in a full fifteen-a-side game. It was suggested that the reduction in performance in the tug-of-war was due to a lack of coordination — they were not all pulling on the rope in unison. However, follow-up studies showed that it may be due to a reduction in motivation rather than a loss of coordination.

Social loafing is when a performer lowers the individual level of effort they contribute to the team. This happens when they believe that they are not a valued member of

> **Social loafing** Refers to individuals reducing their effort/'hiding' when in a team.

the group and their input is going unnoticed, so they stop trying. If the coach does not praise you when you feel you have played well you will eventually give up. Other factors that may cause a performer to loaf include:

- having no clear role within group, for example being unsure of their position within the team
- low self-efficacy/confidence, for example believing that they are not good enough
- learned helplessness (page 45)
- teammates not trying, so they also stop putting in effort — for example, your winger fails to chase a ball, which goes into touch, so you think 'why should I bother?'
- the coach/captain being a poor leader — they do not encourage you and/or employ weak strategies
- experiencing high levels of trait/state anxiety
- injury — for example, you twisted an ankle in training and therefore decide not to bother reaching to return wide serves in tennis
- experiencing social inhibition as a result of an offensive crowd/audience

Strategies to improve cohesion and overcome social loafing in order to enhance team performance include the following:

- highlighting individual performances, for example by giving statistics — shots on target, tackles, assists, etc.
- giving specific roles/responsibilities within the team and ensuring that all members of the team are aware of everyone's roles
- developing social cohesion, for example through team-building exercises, tours and encouraging friendships
- praising/rewarding cohesive behaviour, for example giving encouragement when they work as a team
- raising individuals' confidence/self-efficacy
- encouraging group identity, for example having a set kit
- effective leadership that matches the preferred style of the group
- selecting players who work well together, rather than individual 'stars'
- continually emphasising the team goal
- identifying and avoiding situations where social loafing can occur
- selecting players who are less likely to social loaf
- punishing social loafing
- grooving set plays/focusing on coordination practice

Summary

After studying this topic you should be able to:
- give a clear definition of a group, including interaction, a common goal, mutual awareness and collective identity
- explain how groups are formed, with reference to the four stages of group development (forming, storming, norming and performing)
- explain Steiner's model of group effectiveness (actual productivity = potential productivity − losses due to faulty processes)
- explain the Ringelmann effect, using practical examples
- explain social loafing, using practical examples

Exam tip

Remember to use the correct terminology when referring to Tuckman and Steiner's models in order to access the marks.

Goal setting in sports performance
Importance and effectiveness of goal setting

Performers who set goals are often more successful than those who do not. Psychological research shows that setting goals has positive effects on performance, including:

- giving the performer an aim or focus, allowing them to adopt the correct attentional style
- increasing motivation when the goal is accomplished
- increasing confidence/self-efficacy levels
- controlling arousal/anxiety levels
- monitoring performance to ensure progress is being made
- maintaining **task persistence**
- focusing efforts in training and game situations
- increasing commitment

When setting goals, the SMART principle should be followed (Table 4).

Task persistence
Persevering in efforts to achieve a particular goal.

Table 4 The SMART principle

SMART	Explanation	Example
Specific	The goal must be clear and precise, so that the performer knows what to aim for; it should relate to the performer's role	Netball goal attack to score 90% of goals attempted
Measurable	The goal must be quantifiable, so that progress can be monitored	Aim to reduce 400m time by 2 seconds by end of the season
Achievable	The performer must have the ability to complete the task so that motivation is maintained	The coach sets a relatively experienced runner the target of running 10k in under 60 minutes because they both believe it is possible
Recorded	Attempts to achieve the goal should be documented in order to monitor progress and make adjustments when necessary	The coach records the height of each high jump cleared during training and competition so that if at any point the original goal appears insurmountable, the target can be adjusted
Time phased	A set period must be stated to monitor progress and assess if the goal has been met	Perform a personal best (PB) time in the 100m freestyle swim by the end of next month

Summary

After studying this topic you should be able to:
- explain the importance and effectiveness of goal setting
- explain and give examples of how the SMART principle can be applied (specific, measurable, achievable, recorded and time phased)

Knowledge check 30

What are the key components of the SMART principle?

Attribution

Attribution theory tells us how individuals explain their behaviour. In sport, performers use attributions to offer reasons for why they have won or lost. These reasons, or attributions, will then directly affect the levels of motivation shown in the future.

Weiner's model of attribution

Weiner's model illustrates the following factors within which there are four causal attributions (ability, effort, task difficulty and luck):

- The **locus of causality** — *where* the performer places the reason for the win/loss:
  - **Internal** — within the performer, for example natural *ability* they possess, or *effort* put into training.
  - **External** — outside of the performer/within the environment. For example, *task difficulty* (such as strength of opposition faced) or *luck* (such as decisions made by officials or environmental factors, such as an unlucky ball bounce).
- The **stability dimension** — how *fixed/changeable* the attributions are:
  - **Stable** — relatively permanent. For example, the *ability* (internal, stable) of the performer, which remains the same over time, or the *task difficulty* (external, stable), such as the ability of the opposition.
  - **Unstable** — very changeable. Changes from week to week or even within minutes in a fixture. For example, the *effort* (internal, unstable) is higher when chasing down a ball at the start of the match when taking the lead, than towards the end of the same match when losing. *Luck* (external, unstable) is changeable, for example whether the tennis ball bounces on your side or the opposition's side when it hits the top of the net is down to luck.

Table 5 shows Weiner's suggested classification for these attributions.

Table 5 Weiner's model

		The locus of causality	
		Internal	**External**
The stability dimension	**Stable**	Ability	Task difficulty
	Unstable	Effort	Luck

Weiner later added a third dimension — the **locus of control**. The controllability dimension determines whether or not the performer can control the cause for the win/loss.

- **Personal control** relates to the factors within the performer's control, such as ability and effort. When these attributions are given following successful performances, motivation, pride and satisfaction will increase. However, if internal, stable attributions are used for failure, learned helplessness may occur.
- **External control** relates to uncontrollable factors, such as task difficulty and luck. These attributions can be used to maintain motivation when performers have been unsuccessful. For example, the coach explains that although this game was lost, future games can be won if luck goes their way.

Knowledge check 31

Identify Weiner's four key attributions.

Learned helplessness as a barrier to sports performance

Learned helplessness develops when performers attribute failure internally to stable reasons — for example, I lost the swimming race because I simply do not have the ability. They believe that no matter what they do or how hard they try, they are destined to fail and therefore are not task persistent. This can be either general, relating to all sports (for example, 'I cannot succeed in any sport'), or specific, relating to one skill in sport (for example, 'I cannot take penalty flicks in hockey because I will miss') or a single sport (for example, 'I cannot play badminton'). Individuals who experience learned helplessness may ultimately stop performing completely.

In order to reduce the effects of learned helplessness the performer should change their negative attributions into positive ones. This process is known as **attribution retraining**. Both performers and coaches alike should always attribute the reasons for winning internally to ability and effort (rather than externally to luck), while failure should be attributed externally rather than internally to ability. When coaches and players use correct attributions, motivation will be sustained and performers will increase their task persistence. This also helps to avoid learned helplessness.

Strategies to avoid learned helplessness include the following:

- set realistic process and/or performance goals that enable performers to succeed
- raise self-efficacy (see Bandura's model, page 48)
- highlight previous quality performances
- give positive reinforcement and encouragement to raise confidence
- give demonstrations that are within the player's capability
- use cognitive and somatic stress management techniques, for example imagery or centring

Mastery orientation to optimise performance

Mastery orientation is the opposite of learned helplessness. A performer who is mastery orientated will attribute success to stable and internal factors, such as ability and effort. These performers have a strong belief that they can succeed and will persist even when failing. The performer wishes to excel. This is often a characteristic of high achievers. They also attribute failure to external factors, such as luck and task difficulty, and are able to protect their self-esteem when they are unsuccessful. They utilise **self-serving bias**.

Coaches should aim to generate mastery orientation in their performers in order to improve motivation and sustain confidence. They should ensure that performers attribute losing to external reasons or to unstable/changeable factors — state that task difficulty/luck/low effort were the reasons for the loss. In addition, coaches should highlight effort shown and suggest that with increased effort results can be changed. They should avoid suggesting that losing is due to internal/stable reasons, because this can reduce motivation and cause learned helplessness.

Learned helplessness
The feeling that failure is inevitable. It can be global or specific.

Exam tip

Questions may ask you to describe learned helplessness. Include global and specific examples in your answer.

Knowledge check 32

What is the difference between global and specific learned helplessness?

Self-serving bias
Identifying external and/or unstable reasons for losing, and internal reasons for success.

Summary

After studying this topic you should be able to:
- describe and give examples of Weiner's model of attribution, including the stability dimension (stable and unstable), the locus of causality (internal and external) and the controllability dimension
- explain how learned helplessness can become a barrier to sports performance
- explain how mastery orientation can optimise sports performance

Confidence and self-efficacy in sports performance

Our expectations of whether or not we are going to succeed in sport determine how we approach a task and the levels of effort, motivation and persistence we demonstrate. It is important to understand how confidence impacts on performance, participation and self-esteem.
- **Self-efficacy** is how much belief you have in your ability to achieve goals. It is the belief that you can be successful when carrying out a specific task.
- **Self-confidence** is a general feeling of assurance that you have the ability to meet demands — an absence of doubt.
- **Self-esteem** is how much value you think you have — how positively you regard yourself.

The impact of sports confidence on performance, participation and self-esteem

A performer who has a high level of sports confidence will believe in their ability to achieve and will therefore be motivated to perform. Confident performers are more effective performers. They give appropriate attributions, are able to control their arousal/anxiety levels, are able to deal with an audience being present, can control any aggressive tendencies and have a positive attitude. All of these factors result in a more effective and successful performance.

A confident performer will maintain participation levels because their motivation remains high. The opposite is also true — individuals who have low self-confidence will avoid participating and competing. They may be experiencing learned helplessness and, as a result, lead a sedentary lifestyle.

Individuals with high sports confidence also experience high self-esteem. The general belief in their ability impacts positively on their specific self-efficacy.

Vealey's model of sports confidence

Athletes who have high sports confidence in one sporting situation will feel more confident in their ability to succeed in others. In order to raise confidence levels performers should experience success, so that they will enjoy and continue participating.

Knowledge check 33

Define self-confidence and self-efficacy.

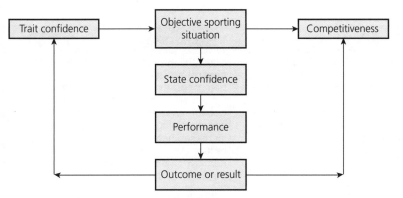

Figure 8 Vealey's model of sports confidence

Vealey's model (Figure 8) suggests that the performer will begin the task, for example taking a conversion in rugby, and perform (behavioural response) with a certain amount of:

- trait sports confidence (SC-trait) — their natural, innate confidence level; for example, they are a generally confident performer
- state sports confidence (SC-state) — their level of confidence in this situation (self-efficacy) is often based on past experience; for example, they are confident that they will score because they have kicked many conversions before
- competitiveness orientation — how competitive the performer is and the types of goal they may have set themselves; for example, the kicker is driven and has set a personal performance goal of scoring 90% of their attempts

The performer produces the response, for example attempts the conversion, and considers the **subjective outcomes**. If they judge the **outcome** as being a positive result, for example they successfully kick the conversion, then the levels of general SC-trait and specific SC-state will **increase**. This will further the chances of approach behaviour being shown in other sporting situations. A successful attempt will also increase the level of competitiveness orientation shown by the performer — for example, the kicker becomes even more motivated and sets a new goal of 95% success rate. A negative outcome will lower trait and state confidence along with competitiveness.

Bandura's theory of self-efficacy

Self-efficacy describes the amount of confidence you have in a particular sporting situation. It is specific rather than general, and varies in different circumstances.

Bandura suggested that four factors can influence the level of self-efficacy shown by a performer. By raising the performer's efficacy levels in one situation to begin with, the coach can increase the performer's self-esteem and belief in their ability to master other tasks.

For example, a young gymnast is experiencing fear when asked to perform on a full-height beam. To increase their self-efficacy the coach should use the four factors shown in Table 6.

Knowledge check 34

According to Vealey, what is SC-state?

Exam tip

In answers relating to Bandura's or Vealey's model, keep the same sporting example throughout and refer to the skill at each stage.

Knowledge check 35

Name the four factors in Bandura's model.

Table 6 Bandura's four factors

Performance accomplishments	Vicarious experiences	Verbal persuasion	Emotional arousal
Remind performers of past success in similar situations For example, remind the gymnast that they were brilliant on the lower beam and that they did not fall off; the width of the higher beam is the same, so they are equally unlikely to fall	Use a **similar role model** who shares characteristics with the performer (for example ability, gender, age) to show that it is possible for them to achieve also For example, ask a gymnast of similar age and standard to perform on the beam; the young gymnast will feel 'if they can do it, so can I'	**Encourage** the performer and tell them that they believe they can succeed; to enhance this, **significant others** should be used For example, the coach and friends of the gymnast persuade them that they believe the gymnast can perform well on the beam	Show the performer how to cope with and **control arousal** levels; this can include both **cognitive** and **somatic** strategies Often performers notice that they have become over-aroused due to psychological and physiological symptoms, for example increased heart rate and sweating; this reduces their self-efficacy because they *perceive* that they are unable to meet the demands of the task For example, the coach tells the performer to use mental rehearsal to go over the moves on the beam in their mind before mounting; this will allow the gymnast to focus and lower their arousal levels

Summary

After studying this topic you should be able to:

- give clear definitions of confidence and self-efficacy
- explain how performance, participation and self-esteem are impacted by sports confidence
- explain each part Vealey's model of sports confidence (including SC-trait, SC-state, competitiveness orientation)
- illustrate Vealey's model with a single practical example; ensure you address each part of the model
- explain each part of Bandura's model of self-efficacy (performance accomplishments, vicarious experiences, verbal persuasion and emotional arousal)
- illustrate Bandura's model with a single practical example; ensure you address each part of the model

Leadership in sport

Characteristics of effective leaders

Effective leaders:

- have a clear vision or goal
- have effective communication skills
- are ambitious
- are motivators/motivated
- are charismatic
- are knowledgeable about the sport/skilful
- are empathetic
- are confident
- are adaptable

Emergent or prescribed leaders

Prescribed leaders are chosen from outside the group. For example, national governing bodies appoint national team managers. They often bring new ideas to the group but can cause disagreements if the group members are opposed to the appointment.

Emergent leaders are selected from within the group, often because they are nominated by the other group members. For example, a Sunday league football team votes the previous season's 'players' player' as its new captain. There is already a high level of respect for this person, but if they have had the same experiences as the other team members, they may not be able to bring any new strategies to enable the team to progress.

Knowledge check 36

What is the difference between prescribed and emergent leaders?

Leadership styles

A leader can choose from a range of styles (Table 7).

Table 7 Styles of leadership

An autocratic/task-orientated leader	A democratic/socially orientated leader	A laissez-faire leader
■ Adopts a dictatorial style ■ Is only interested in ensuring that the task is fulfilled ■ Is the sole decision maker ■ Is preferred by male performers ■ Uses this style: 　■ in dangerous situations 　■ with large groups 　■ if time is limited 　■ with hostile groups 　■ with cognitive performers	■ Is interested in ensuring that relationships are developed within the group ■ Encourages the group members to be involved in making decisions ■ Is preferred by female performers ■ Uses this style: 　■ with small groups 　■ if there is a lot of time available 　■ with friendly groups 　■ with advanced performers	■ Is more of a 'figurehead' than an active leader ■ Allows the group members to make all the decisions ■ Is useful if a problem-solving approach is required ■ Is only effective with advanced performers

Theories of leadership

The trait approach — the 'great man' theory

This approach suggests that leaders are born with the necessary characteristics to become a good leader. The theory states that characteristics are **innate** and are shown by males rather than females. The genetic leadership qualities are stable and enduring, meaning that they will be shown equally in all situations. There is little support for this theory because it is rare to find an individual who can lead effectively in and outside of the sporting arena. It also does not accept the effects of the environment or that individuals can learn the necessary qualities to become an effective leader. There are also many successful female leaders.

Social learning theory

This approach opposes the trait theory, leading to the 'nature versus nurture' debate. Social learning theory suggests that leaders are not born with their skills, but that individuals learn them from experience. They develop their leadership skills by observing and imitating other successful leaders. For example, they may see how their team captain is able to successfully motivate players with authoritative team talks, which spurs them on to win. The performer recognises that the leader is effective and therefore copies their leadership style.

Knowledge check 37

Name the three styles of leadership.

Exam tip

A common mistake made by students is to confuse *styles* of leadership with the *theories* of leadership. Ensure that you read the question multiple times to work out what is required in your answer.

Interactionist approach

This is the most widely accepted approach because it combines both the trait and social learning theories of leadership. It suggests that leaders are born with the necessary leadership traits, but they also learn and develop other characteristics through experience.

Chelladurai's multidimensional model of leadership

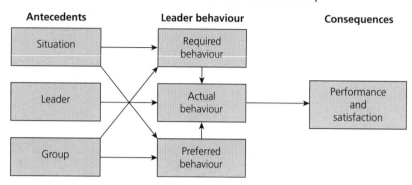

Figure 9 The Chelladurai model of leadership

Chelladurai's model suggests that the leader must be able to **adapt** their leadership style. They must consider three factors:

- The **situation**, such as the strength of the opponents or if there is any danger involved. For example, learning to trampoline is dangerous and requires an autocratic approach.
- The **leader**, including their ability, personality and preferred leadership style. For example, the leader is highly experienced and prefers to use an autocratic style.
- The **group**, including their ability levels, and the relationships with each other and the leader. For example, the group comprises cognitive performers who therefore need to be given direct instructions about how to perform moves on the trampoline bed.

The leadership style is also affected by the following:

- **Required behaviour**, for example what the situation demands. A dangerous task such as trampolining would require an autocratic rather than democratic approach in order to maintain safety levels.
- **Actual behaviour**, for example what style and approach the leader decides to take. This is based on their own characteristics, such as ability. For example, the leader considers all the factors and decides to use an autocratic style of leadership.
- **Preferred behaviour**, for example what style of leadership the performers would like best, and is based on their own characteristics, such as ability. For example, the group likes the autocratic approach because they can develop their basic skills and can therefore move onto more difficult skills quickly.

Once these factors have been considered, the leader must try to align their style of leadership with each of these in order to gain the highest level of performance and satisfaction from the group. The more the leader's actual behaviour matches what the group wants and what the situation needs, the better the performance will be. In the example given above, the leader decides to use the autocratic style. As this matches

> **Exam tip**
>
> Students often find describing Chelladurai's model difficult. Keep the same example throughout and refer to it when explaining each part of the model. Try working backwards through the model.

what the group likes and what the situation needs, there is a greater chance that performance will improve and that the group will be satisfied.

Summary

After studying this topic you should be able to:
- give characteristics of an effective leader
- describe the three styles of leadership (autocratic, democratic and laissez-faire)
- define and give examples of prescribed and emergent leaders
- describe the three theories of leadership (trait, social learning and interactionist)
- explain Chelladurai's model, illustrating it with sporting examples

Stress management to optimise performance

Definition and causes of stress

Stress is how an individual responds to a threat. Stress is a negative response, which causes anxiety, for example experiencing negative thoughts prior to a local derby.

Eustress is a positive response to a threat, for example feeling that you can overcome the challenge of completing a difficult rock climb.

Stressors include:
- task importance, for example final/local derby
- injury/fear of injury
- fear of failure
- social inhibition
- pressure from coach
- pressure to achieve extrinsic rewards, for example prize money/sponsorship
- high-level opponents

Cognitive effects of stress are psychological, for example negative/irrational thoughts.

Somatic effects of stress are physiological, for example increased heart rate and blood pressure, and feeling nauseous.

Use of cognitive stress management techniques

There are various cognitive techniques that can be used to manage stress:
- **Mental rehearsal** — going over the performance in your mind. For example, seeing all the subroutines of the triple jump in your mind, without moving.
- **Imagery** — recalling a successful previous performance and using all the senses, including kinaesthesis, to recreate the feeling of success. For example, remembering how the serve felt when you hit an ace.
- **Positive thinking/self-talk** — verbally reminding yourself of the key points of the movement and telling yourself that you can achieve your goal. For example, a rugby league player taking a conversion will talk himself through the run up, contact and follow through. He will tell himself that he can take the points. He might also have a mantra or saying that he continually repeats.

Knowledge check 38

What is the difference between stress and eustress?

Knowledge check 39

How do cognitive and somatic effects of stress differ?

- **Negative-thought stopping** — often used with the above approaches. For example, a tennis player whose first serve is letting them down and begins to think 'I can't hit one in', should replace that thought with, 'I can and I will hit the next one in'.
- **Rational thinking** — any negative thoughts that come into the performer's mind should be challenged with logical thoughts. This makes the performer feel more in control.
- **Goal setting** — using the SMART principle (page 43) can improve confidence, motivation and reduce stress because the performer has a clear aim.
- **Mindfulness** — the performer focuses their attention on the present. They accept their thoughts and feelings in a calm, controlled way. They recognise the stressors and can deal positively with their emotions.

Use of somatic stress management techniques

Somatic stress management techniques include the following:

- **Progressive muscular relaxation** — concentrating on each muscle group in turn. By tensing, holding and then relaxing each group the performer begins to relax.
- **Biofeedback** — using equipment, for example a heart rate monitor that displays bpm, while the performer tries various stress management strategies. The resulting physiological data will show which is the best method for them. These strategies are effective, but are time-consuming. Using equipment during performance can distract athletes and increases anxiety levels because they are aware that they are being monitored.
- **Breathing control** — by controlling and concentrating on the rate and depth of breathing the performer becomes less distracted, allowing them to focus on the task.
- **Centring** — concentrating fully on their body (often the centre — the belly-button region), the performer breathes in. As they breathe out, they chant a word or phrase relating to how they wish to perform — strong, focused, calm, etc. By doing this they maintain focus on themselves and any negative thoughts are disregarded. It is often used alongside controlled breathing and is useful during breaks in performance, such as timeouts or the end of a tennis set.

Summary

After studying this topic you should be able to:
- define stress
- describe the causes of stress
- explain how cognitive and somatic stress management techniques can be used to optimise performance

Questions & Answers

This section explains the structure of OCR A-level Paper H555/02, and discusses strategies for approaching the different types of question you will encounter. This is followed by a series of sample questions covering all the question types — multiple choice, short answer and extended writing. Each question is followed by a sample student answer, with accompanying comments. You should practise all the questions yourself and then compare your answers with the sample student answers. Be sure to read the comments on the answers to improve your understanding of what is required to achieve full marks. An effective revision strategy is to take each of the Student B answers, read the comments on them and then rewrite the answer so that they achieve full marks.

Exam format

Paper 2 is a 60-mark paper that is worth 20% of your A-level. It has three sections. Section A comprises five compulsory 2-mark questions worth a total of 10 marks. Section B comprises a selection of compulsory questions ranging from 1 to 6 marks and is worth a total of 40 marks. Section C is a compulsory extended open-response question. This is worth 10 marks. Section C will be marked using a levels-based mark scheme.

The time allowed for the examination is 1 hour.

The extended-writing question is marked using banded marking criteria. Your examiner will not just count the number of assessment objective (AO) marks. They will also assess quality of written communication. They will use a grid and highlight your answers using the following categories to come to an overall judgement. When a question is marked with an asterisk (*) your extended answer will be assessed for the following:

- AO1 — knowledge and understanding
- AO2 — application, supported by examples
- AO3 — analysis/evaluation
- relevant terminology/specialist vocabulary
- line of reasoning, clarity, structure and focus

(In the sample answers to extended-response questions in this section, each assessment objective has been labelled (AO1, AO2 and AO3), so it is easier for you to see where the answer demonstrates knowledge and understanding, application and analysis/evaluation.)

In your extended answer you are required to draw together knowledge from more than one topic in this component, and show how the topics relate to each other. The best way to structure your answer to this type of question is to make a relevant knowledge point (AO1), develop/analyse it (AO3) and give a relevant practical example to support your answer (AO2).

Finally, in the exam it is important that you write clearly in the spaces provided in the answer booklet. Avoid writing anything that you want to be marked in the margins, and always indicate if you run out of space that your answer continues on additional paper or at the end of the answer booklet if there is space. Make sure that it is clear to the examiner which question you are answering on the additional paper. Include question and part numbers.

Comments

Each question is followed by a brief analysis of what to watch out for when answering the question. All student responses are then accompanied by comments indicating where credit is due. In the weaker answers, they also point out areas for improvement, specific problems and common errors, such as lack of clarity, weak or non-existent development, irrelevance, misinterpretation of the question and mistaken meanings of terms.

Skill acquisition

Classification of skills

Question 1

With reference to the continua identified below, classify the skill of a pass in ice hockey. You must justify your answers:

[4 marks]

- continuity
- difficulty
- environmental influence
- muscular involvement

> To access all 4 marks you must classify the ice hockey pass correctly on each of the continua identified, and then justify your answers. You must make it clear which of the continua you are describing.

Student A

A pass in ice hockey can be classified as discrete on the continuity continuum. It can be classified as complex on the difficulty continuum. It can be classified as an open skill on the environmental influence continuum. Finally, it can be classified as gross on the muscular involvement continuum.

The pass is a discrete skill because it has a clear beginning (when the stick is swung backwards preparing to hit the puck) and a clear ending when the player finishes the follow through with their stick ✓. If the player wants to repeat the pass, they must start from the beginning each time.

The pass is a complex skill because when producing the pass, the player has to make several decisions in order to complete it, including who to pass to ✓, where the defenders are, and the direction, speed, power and trajectory of the pass.

It is classified as an open skill because the environment around the player is constantly changing. Their team mates are continually moving around the ice ✓ in order to get into position to receive the pass, and the opposition team members are also moving and attempting to block or intercept the pass. The player must consider all of the environmental actions and adapt to what is happening around them.

Finally, the pass is a gross skill because it involves the use of large muscle groups in the body. When the player strikes the puck they will use large muscle groups in the back and legs ✓ as well as in the arms in order to produce the pass.

> Student A has given an excellent answer to this question on classification. Classification questions appear regularly on exam papers. In the first paragraph, Student A has correctly classified the ice hockey pass on all four of the continua that have been identified. At this point the student has not gained any credit, because they have not yet justified the answer. However, this is an effective introduction to the rest of their answer. In each of the subsequent paragraphs, Student A justifies clearly and methodically *why* they have classified the ice hockey pass as such on each of the continua. **4/4 marks awarded**

Student B

The pass is open because the performer adapts to receive the pass. In terms of continuity it is a serial skill because all the parts of the pass are put together and run in order. It is a simple skill on the difficulty continua. It is a gross skill in terms of muscular involvement because it uses big muscle groups, such as the hamstrings and the trapezius ✓.

Student B has offered a very brief answer for the 4 marks on offer. They have correctly identified that the pass is open and the justification is correct, however, it is not clear which of the continua this relates to and therefore credit cannot be given.

Student B has incorrectly classified the ice hockey pass as serial on the continuity continuum. It is a discrete skill that has a clear beginning and ending. The explanation of a serial skill is correct, but this classification relates to skills such as dance sequences and the triple jump.

They have incorrectly classified the skill as simple on the difficulty continuum. Simple skills require few decisions, for example the forward roll.

Finally, Student B gains credit for the correct classification and justification of the pass on the muscular involvement continuum. **1/4 marks awarded**

Question 2

Classify *two* different skills in your sport using both extremes on the pacing continuum. [2 marks]

With only 2 marks on offer, you have to correctly describe the extremes of the pacing continuum (using your AO1 skills) *and* give an accurate practical example (using your AO2 skills) from your sport.

Student A

A self-paced skill is when the performer controls the rate, speed and timing of the skill. In my sport of football, I would classify taking a shot on goal as a self-paced skill. This is because I decide how fast and when to take the shot ✓. I would classify receiving a pass as an externally paced skill. Externally paced skills are when the rate, speed and timing of the skill are not controlled by me — they are controlled by the environment. As the ball is coming towards me, I have no control over how fast it is travelling or the direction it is travelling in. I have to adapt, making it externally paced ✓.

For both self- and externally paced skills, Student A gives a clear description of the classification and illustrates both answers with accurate examples from their sport, football. There is a lot to do to gain each of the marks and Student A demonstrates how this can be done in a succinct way. **2/2 marks awarded**

Student B

My sport is netball. When I play goal attack and take a penalty shot, this is a self-paced skill because the pace of the shot is dictated by me. Self-paced skills are when the pace is controlled by the performer.

When I perform a bounce pass, this is an externally paced skill.

Student B's example of taking a penalty shot is correct. However, in the description of the self-paced skill, the student has used the word 'pace'. This is a repeat of the question and therefore will not be credited. Make sure you find alternative ways of saying 'pace', such as rate/speed.

The example of performing a bounce pass is incorrect because this too would be a self-paced skill. Student B has also not described the classification and therefore fails to score. **0/2 marks awarded**

Types and methods of practice

Question 3

Describe the whole method of presentation. With reference to performers' experience and skill classification, evaluate its effectiveness when developing skills.*

[10 marks]

This is an extended synoptic question, worth 10 marks, that requires you to draw together knowledge from practice and classification, so you need to access as many AO1, AO2 and AO3 marks as you can. Remember that this is a banded mark question, so your answer is considered holistically. One correct answer does not mean 1 mark. Show your knowledge and understanding of the whole method of practice, identify, classify and justify sporting skills, and finally evaluate how effective the whole method would be in developing them. Remember that your quality of written communication is also assessed as part of the answer.

Student A

The whole method of presentation means that the skill is not broken down into its subroutines AO1. It is presented in its entirety AO1. The whole method could be used with highly organised skills, which are difficult to break down into subroutines AO1, such as the golf swing AO2. It can also be used with continuous skills that do not have a clear beginning and ending AO1, such as cycling AO2. Simple skills such as the forward roll AO2 can be presented in their entirety because there are few decisions to make AO1 when performing.

It is advantageous to use the whole method with highly organised skills because it maintains fluency AO3 between the subroutines of the skill. For example, practising the full tennis serve rather than parts, such as the ball toss AO2, ensures that kinaesthesis AO3 is developed. It is not time-consuming AO3, so a full tennis serve can be produced in a small amount of time, and it enables the performer to develop a clear mental image AO3 of what the tennis serve should look like. However, it is difficult to use with cognitive performers AO3 because they can become overloaded, so other methods such as progressive-part practice should be utilised. It can be used effectively with autonomous performers because they have a good understanding of the skill as a whole, for example an autonomous sprinter knows what to do in the sprint start AO2 and can produce it fully each time. It is also quite fatiguing AO3 to repeatedly produce the full skill. For example, you would be extremely tired having to do a full somersault AO2 over and over; therefore, the performer must be physically capable of producing the full skill AO3.

This answer covers all the assessment objectives and would score in the top band. Student A has accurately described the whole method of presentation. They have classified and justified several sporting skills that would be best presented using the whole method, and have evaluated the method, giving clear advantages and disadvantages that explain its effectiveness.
10/10 marks awarded

Student B

This means the skill is presented as one **AO1**, for example showing the full cartwheel **AO2**. A cartwheel is hard to break down into parts because it is highly organised **AO1**. It is a quick method to use **AO3**.

The whole method should be used if the skill does not have a definite start and end **AO1** because it is cyclic, like the badminton smash.

> This is a weak answer. Knowledge of the whole method is limited and there is little application to sporting situations. A basic analysis mark has been awarded; other than this, there is no analysis/evaluation.
> **4/10 marks awarded**

Question 4

What is fixed practice and with which classification of skills would you use this method?

[3 marks]

> This is a typical two-part question and you must address both parts to access all the available marks. First, state clearly what fixed practice is for 1 mark. Second, you should identify which of the skill classifications you would use this method with. You must give at least two skill classifications to hit full marks. However, using the best exam technique, you should aim for three. The examiners apply 'positive marking' methods, so you should always try to give more answers than there are marks available.

Student A

Fixed practice means that the performer practises the same skill, repeatedly ✓ in a stable environment. The skill is repeated over and over, without adjustments.

Fixed practice should be used with closed skills ✓ because they are unaffected by the environment. It is also used with simple skills ✓ because the decision-making element is low. If the skill is self-paced, fixed practice can also be used.

> A clear and accurate definition gains the first mark. Two further marks are given for correctly stating that closed and simple skills can use this practice method. The application to self-paced skills is also a correct answer, but maximum marks have already been achieved. **3/3 marks awarded**

Student B

Fixed practice is repeating the same skill in the same way over and over ✓. It can be used with self-paced skills ✓.

> A clear definition is given to access the first mark. Only one further answer is offered to describe which classification of skills it is used for. Addition of a further classification would have reached full marks.
> **2/3 marks awarded**

Transfer of skills

Question 5

Which one of the following describes negative transfer? Put a tick (✓) in the box next
to the correct answer.

[1 mark]

A   Negative transfer is when one skill aids the learning and performance of another skill.

☐

B   Negative transfer is when you learn to perform a skill on the left side of the body
and then do the same on the right side of the body.

☐

C   Negative transfer is when there are no transferrable elements between two skills.

☐

D   Negative transfer is when one skill hinders the learning and performance of another skill.

☐

> There may be multiple-choice questions in your exam. Ensure that you follow the
> instructions on how to answer this type of question carefully. If the question asks for a
> tick in the box, do not put a cross or circle it.

Student A

A   Negative transfer is when one skill aids the learning
and performance of another skill.

☐

B   Negative transfer is when you learn to perform a skill
on the left side of the body and then do the same on
the right side of the body.

☐

C   Negative transfer is when there are no transferrable
elements between two skills.

☐

D   Negative transfer is when one skill hinders the learning
and performance of another skill.

✓

Student A has correctly identified
negative transfer from the options
available and has ticked the box as per
the instructions in the question. Make
sure you learn the definitions of all five
types of transfer carefully.
1/1 mark awarded

Student B

A   Negative transfer is when one skill aids the learning
and performance of another skill.

☐

B   Negative transfer is when you learn to perform a skill
on the left side of the body and then do the same on
the right side of the body.

✗

C   Negative transfer is when there are no transferrable
elements between two skills.

☐

D   Negative transfer is when one skill hinders the learning
and performance of another skill.

☐

Student B has incorrectly identified
definition B, which is bilateral transfer.
They have also used a cross rather than
a tick as requested in the question.
Make sure you read every question
carefully and follow the instructions.
0/1 mark awarded

Question 6

How would a coach encourage positive transfer?

[4 marks]

> This requires you to describe at least four ways of ensuring that positive transfer occurs. It does not ask you to give a practical example, but it is always useful to link your theoretical knowledge to sporting skills to help demonstrate your understanding to the examiner.

Student A

There are several strategies that a coach can use to ensure that positive transfer occurs. Firstly, the coach should structure practices that ensure that the performer's first skill is grooved ✓. When comparing two skills, the coach should highlight ✓ to the performer where positive transfer can take place. For example, the coach points out the similarities between the subroutines of the tennis serve and those of the volleyball serve. The coach should also make sure that the practice environment ✓ for both skills is as similar as possible and that the practice sessions are as close to a game ✓ situation as they can be. Finally, when the performer is successful in transferring skills, the coach should offer praise and positive reinforcement.

This is a strong answer that accesses all of the AO3 marks available. Student A effectively describes five strategies that a coach can use to ensure that positive transfer takes place. The last point is not credited because the answer has already achieved the maximum score. It is good exam technique to give more answers than there are marks available. A good practical example is used to support this answer, even though it is not required. **4/4 marks awarded**

Student B

Positive transfer is when one skill helps the learning and performance of another. For example, learning how to do an overarm throw will help you with your overarm fielding throws in cricket. The coach should make sure that the overarm throw is learned fully and grooved before trying to teach the fielding technique ✓. This will stop negative transfer from happening. Negative transfer is when one skill hinders the learning and performance of another skill. For example, learning the 'footwork' rule in netball hinders your performance in basketball because when you are passed the ball you automatically stop rather than dribble.

Student B has made two common mistakes. First, the definition and a good practical example of what positive transfer is have been given. Although what Student B has written is correct, this is a waste of time and will be marked as irrelevant by the examiner. The second mistake is to include a definition and example of negative transfer, which is also irrelevant. Read each question multiple times to be certain of what the question is asking you to do. **1/4 marks awarded**

Principles and theories of learning movement skills
Question 7

Describe the cognitive theory of learning and use practical examples to support your answer. What are the disadvantages of using this method to learn sporting skills?   [6 marks]

This question needs you to explain the key concepts in the cognitive theory of learning and link them to examples. Do not confuse the cognitive theory of learning with the cognitive phase of learning — this is a common mistake. To access all of the marks available, you must address all parts of the question and include practical examples. There will be a sub-max applied to this question. You will only be able to gain credit for four theory points and therefore you need to aim for at least two disadvantages of using this method to gain full marks.

Student A

The cognitive theory of learning suggests that performers learn best when the skill is presented to them, and they are allowed to practise it, as a whole ✓. When learning the tennis serve, the coach will present the full skill rather than individual subroutines. Cognitive theorists suggest that the performer uses insight ✓ in order to work out what to do. They will also use their past experiences ✓ to help them in the current situation. They may, for example, use their memory of the overarm throw to help them to perform the tennis serve.

This theory also suggests that there are intervening variables ✓, which means the performer has to mentally process what happens between the stimulus and response. For example, they will process that when the ball is at its highest point during the ball toss (stimulus) the correct action is to strike it at this point (response). The learner will also use their judgement or perception to help them to learn. They will make judgements on the correct power and speed with which to hit the ball so that it lands in the service box. However, performing the whole tennis serve might be too difficult for cognitive performers, and they may experience information overload ✓. They might also become fatigued. If the skill is dangerous, it might not be possible to use this method because they might become injured ✓.

This is an excellent answer. Student A has addressed all parts of the question and as a result has accessed all the available marks. The descriptions of the key parts of the cognitive theory of learning are clear and supported by practical examples. As there is a sub-max allocated to this question, only four theory points are credited despite Student A giving more than four correct answers. The answer also includes correct disadvantages of using this method to learn skills.
6/6 marks awarded

Student B

The cognitive theory of learning says that the performer's movements will be slow and jerky. For example, when learning a dance sequence the movements do not flow with each other. The dancer will also make lots of mistakes such as not landing their jumps correctly. Performers also rely heavily on extrinsic feedback from the coach, such as telling them how to spot their turns.

Student B has completely misread the question and has made the common mistake of writing about the cognitive stage of learning, rather than the cognitive theory of learning. Make a note to yourself in your class notes to avoid this happening to you. Read every question more than once to ensure that you are clear on what the question is asking you to do. **0/6 marks awarded**

Question 8

Bandura suggests that performers learn through observation. Describe how a performer would learn to dribble in hockey, with reference to the attention and motivation parts of his model.

[4 marks]

This question requires a good understanding of Bandura's model. You need to apply your knowledge to get all the marks on offer. Show how the 'attention' and 'motivation' parts of the model would help a performer to learn to dribble.

Student A

Bandura states that the performer must pay attention and be motivated in order to learn to dribble. The hockey player should focus on the key aspects ✓ of the skill. The coach can highlight the main parts. For example, the coach will point out exactly where the player's hands should be ✓ as they grip the hockey stick. In addition, the player must be driven ✓ to learn how to dribble and have the desire to practise the skill of dribbling ✓.

Both parts of the model have been correctly described and an example related to dribbling in hockey given to support each answer. It is clear that Student A understands Bandura's model. **4/4 marks awarded**

Student B

Bandura says that the performer must pay attention to the stick and ball. This means that they have to remember how the dribble is supposed to be done and have a clear mental image of the dribble. The performer must really want ✓ to do the skill too.

This answer shows that Student B has some understanding of Bandura's model but does not appear to have revised enough. They have written about 'remembering/having a clear image of the skill', which relates to a different part of the model (retention). This is a common mistake. No mark can be offered for the example here. This response scrapes 1 mark for describing motivation, but has not offered an example so no further credit can be given. **1/4 marks awarded**

Stages of learning

Question 9

A football player has recently joined a team and has become increasingly more proficient in their skills. Using an example from football, describe the associative stage of learning.

[4 marks]

The question requires a description of the associative stage only. You must give an example from football to support your answer.

Student A

The footballer has continually practised ✓ their dribbling ✓ skills in order to progress from the cognitive phase. Their dribbling is much smoother ✓, and they can start to look up a bit to the other players in their surrounding environment ✓ rather than just focusing on the ball. If they do not practise regularly, they might not progress on to the next stage, which is the autonomous stage.

This answer makes more than enough scoring points, by giving more than three correct descriptive points for the associative stage and a simple but effective example from football, as requested. **4/4 marks awarded**

Student B

They make fewer mistakes when playing football. They start to develop kinaesthesis ✓ of the movements. They might not go any further.

Student B has made some attempt to answer the question and has scored 1 mark for a correct technical word. However, 'fewer mistakes' is already implied in the question ('more proficient') and therefore cannot be credited. 'When playing football' is also too vague to gain the example point — Student B should have named a skill, for example passing or shooting, and linked it to a description of the associative phase. **1/4 marks awarded**

Guidance

Question 10

Which one of the following is an example of manual guidance? Put a tick (✓) in the box next to the correct answer.

[1 mark]

A   The performer watches a video of a footballer passing.

B   The coach stands behind the golfer with their arms around them. The coach places their hands on top of the golfer's and supports their swing.

C   A young child uses stabilisers on their new bike.

D   A tennis coach explains how to successfully perform the drop shot.

Multiple-choice questions may appear to be easy but they can be tricky. Do not rush into answering — read the question several times before you tick the box.

Student A

A   The performer watches a video of a footballer passing.

B   The coach stands behind the golfer with their arms around them. The coach places their hands on top of the golfer's and supports their swing. ✓

C   A young child uses stabilisers on their new bike.

D   A tennis coach explains how to successfully perform the drop shot.

The student has correctly identified the example of manual guidance. Make sure you can describe all four types of guidance and give clear sporting examples of each.
1/1 mark awarded

Student B

A   The performer watches a video of a footballer passing.   ☐

B   The coach stands behind the golfer with their arms around them. The coach places their hands on top of the golfer's and supports their swing.   ☐

C   A young child uses stabilisers on their new bike.   ✓

D   A tennis coach explains how to successfully perform the drop shot.   ☐

Student B has made the common mistake of confusing manual guidance with mechanical guidance. Read the question carefully.
0/1 mark awarded

Question 11

Other than manual guidance, identify *two* other types of guidance. What factors would you take into account when you decide on the most effective method of guidance to use?

[4 marks]

This is another two-part question so you must address both parts of the question to access all the available marks. A common mistake is to miss one of the two parts out. Ensure that you identify two other types of guidance and describe at least two factors that you would consider before using guidance methods.

Student A

Two other types of guidance are verbal guidance ✓ and visual guidance ✓. When deciding on the most effective method of guidance to use, you should always be aware of the classification and type of skill ✓ — for example, if is there danger involved. You should also consider the stage of learning ✓ that the performer is at. For example, you would use mechanical guidance more frequently with a cognitive performer than you would with an autonomous performer.

This is a good answer. Two additional guidance types are identified in the first part of the answer. The second part clearly and succinctly describes the factors to be considered before selecting a guidance method.
4/4 marks awarded

Student B

Two other types of guidance are physical and mechanical ✓. The performer's experience ✓ should be considered.

This is too brief for a question that has 4 marks allocated to it. It suggests that Student B was running out of time. You should spend roughly 1 minute for each mark that is available on the paper. Student B has also mistakenly used the word 'physical' to identify a type of guidance. This is a common mistake that students make when describing manual guidance.
2/4 marks awarded

Question 12

What are the disadvantages of using verbal guidance? [4 marks]

This question is straightforward provided you read it carefully. You must only write about the type of guidance identified and only give the *disadvantages* associated with that type of guidance. Common mistakes made by students when answering these types of questions (and therefore wasting valuable time) include defining the guidance type, writing about visual, manual or mechanical guidance and/or including advantages of the type of guidance.

Student A

The disadvantages of using verbal guidance are that it is difficult to use with cognitive performers/beginners ✓ because they may not understand the technical information given by the coach ✓. Also, if the verbal instructions are not correct, the performer might not produce the correct movements ✓. If too many instructions are given at once, the performer might experience information overload ✓. For example, it may not be effective to describe all the parts of a ten-bounce routine in trampolining to a cognitive learner, as they may not be able to remember all the parts and feel overwhelmed with the information.

This is a strong answer that is gains all the credit available. Student A effectively describes four disadvantages of verbal guidance. A good practical example is used to support the answer, even though it is not required.
4/4 marks awarded

Student B

Verbal guidance is giving the performer instructions or an explanation of how to perform the skill or what tactics are needed. This is good to use with autonomous performers and is quick and efficient. However, it might be better to use visual guidance such as a demonstration ✓ instead of verbal guidance, especially if the skill is complex. Also, by just using verbal guidance the performer may become bored ✓.

Student B has not read the question properly and as a result has included irrelevant information and missed out on 2 valuable marks. There is no requirement to define verbal guidance or to give advantages.
2/4 marks awarded

Feedback

Question 13

Give *two* benefits of giving feedback.

[2 marks]

> This is a straightforward question that you might encounter in Section A. As the question specifies *two* benefits, the examiner will only mark the first two answers that you give.

Student A

The benefits of giving feedback are that it can correct any errors ✓ that the performer may make, and can also be motivational for them ✓.

> This answer is clear and to the point, accessing both available marks.
> **2/2 marks awarded**

Student B

It is good to give feedback because:

1 it reinforces what the performer is doing correctly ✓
2 it is extrinsic
3 it improves confidence

> Student B has given three answers to this question. They gain credit for point 1, but point 2 is a type of feedback rather than a benefit and therefore cannot be credited. The third answer is correct, but because the question specifies *two* benefits, the examiner will only mark the first two answers. If the question had simply said 'Give the benefits', then this answer would have been credited too. You must be fully informed about the different ways in which questions can be asked.
> **1/2 marks awarded**

Question 14

What are the advantages and disadvantages of using the knowledge of performance method of feedback?

[4 marks]

> This is another two-part question. To access all the available marks, give two advantages of knowledge of performance and two disadvantages. Common mistakes made by students when answering these types of questions include defining the feedback type, writing about advantages *or* disadvantages and not both, and/or writing about other types of feedback that are irrelevant, which wastes valuable time.

Student A

One advantage of using knowledge of performance is that the coach can tell the performer how to improve ✓. It can also be used to motivate the performer ✓ and to give them confidence. However, the disadvantages are that too much information can be given all at once, which might cause information overload ✓. Also, the performer might only want to know the outcome ✓, so knowledge of results should be used.

> This is an excellent and succinct answer that offers two advantages and two disadvantages of knowledge of performance.
> **4/4 marks awarded**

Student B

The advantage of using knowledge of performance is that the coach can tell the performer about the outcome at the end of their performance and therefore does not distract them.

The disadvantages are that it can lower the performer's confidence and it doesn't tell them which aspects of their action to improve.

> Student B has made the common mistake of confusing knowledge of results with knowledge of performance. You must read the question carefully so that you don't make similar mistakes.
> **0/4 marks awarded**

Memory models

Question 15

A gymnast performing on a beam has to use selective attention because their competitors are performing on other pieces of apparatus in the competition venue at the same time. With reference to gymnastics, describe what selective attention is and explain how it benefits the performer.

[4 marks]

> There are several points to address in this question. You must describe selective attention and give an example that relates to gymnastics. To access all the marks, you must then explain the benefits of selective attention.

Student A

Selective attention acts as an information filter. The performer will focus on the relevant stimuli in the environment and disregard the irrelevant information ✓. The gymnast will only be focusing on landing their moves on the beam and will completely ignore the other performers on the floor/vault, etc. and the shouts from the crowd ✓. This will benefit them because it will control their arousal/ anxiety levels ✓ and stop their from becoming distracted ✓. The gymnast will be able to concentrate fully.

> This answer makes more than enough scoring points. Student A has described selective attention clearly and has given a clear example relating to gymnastics, as required by the question. Finally, a number of benefits are explained, so all the available marks have been awarded. **4/4 marks awarded**

Student B

The gymnast will selectively attend, so they will focus on the beam and not on the gymnast next to them on the uneven bars ✓. This will benefit the gymnast as they will not experience information overload ✓.

> Student B has not addressed all parts of the question — selective attention is not described. This is a common mistake in exams. Make sure that you highlight the questions so that you address each part before moving on. This answer gives a good example and one benefit. To access all the marks, other benefits of selective attention should have been given.
> **2/4 marks awarded**

Sports psychology

Individual differences: personality

Question 16

As part of the trait approach, psychologists have suggested two personality types. Type A performers are likely to experience stress, whereas type B performers are said to be less likely to experience stress.

Identify *one* other characteristic of type A performers and one other characteristic of type B performers.

[2 marks]

> The question requires knowledge and understanding of type A and type B personalities. To access both marks, give one characteristic of each personality type.

Student A

Type A personalities work fast ✓ and type B personalities are tolerant ✓ of others.

> Student A offers a correct characteristic of type A personalities and a different characteristic relating to type B personalities.
> **2/2 marks awarded**

Student B

Type A personalities experience high anxiety and type B personalities are less competitive than others ✓.

> Student B has made the common mistake of rephrasing the question. Anxiety and stress would be classed as the same marking point and therefore another characteristic must be given to access the mark.
> **1/2 marks awarded**

Question 17

Identify the correct equation used to illustrate the interactionist approach to personality. Put a tick (✓) in the box next to the correct answer.

[1 mark]

A $P = f(D \times H)$

B $B = f(T \times E)$

C $P = f(D \times E)$

D $B = f(P \times E)$

> The question requires you to know the correct equation. There will be multiple-choice questions in your exam so you need to follow the instructions on how to answer these carefully.

Student A

A $P = f(D \times H)$

B $B = f(T \times E)$

C $P = f(D \times E)$

D $B = f(P \times E)$ ✓

> D is correct. Behaviour is a function of genetic personality traits and experiences gained through social learning. **1/1 mark awarded**

Student B

A $P = f(D \times H)$

B $B = f(T \times E)$

C $P = f(D \times E)$

D $B = f(P \times E)$ ✗

> This answer is correct, but Student B has not followed the instructions. They have used a cross instead of a tick and therefore do not gain credit. Make sure you do not make silly mistakes like this and give easy marks away.
> **0/1 mark awarded**

Individual differences: attitudes

Question 18

Identify the components of an attitude. How can a young person demonstrate a positive attitude towards pre-season training?

[6 marks]

> This question has 3 AO1 and 3 AO2 marks available. To access all 6 marks, ensure that you use the correct terminology when identifying the three components of an attitude. Then link your theoretical knowledge of each component to the example of pre-season training.

Student A

The triadic model says that there are three components in an attitude. The first one is the cognitive component ✓. This is the performer's thoughts and beliefs in relation to the attitude object. The second component is the affective part ✓. This is the way the performer feels. It is their emotional response to the attitude object. Finally, there is the behavioural component ✓. This is the way that the performer acts. It is their physical response towards the attitude object.

A young person can demonstrate a positive attitude towards pre-season training by thinking positively about it. Their cognitive

> Student A scores full marks for a well-structured answer. The first paragraph shows knowledge and understaanding of the three attitude components. All 3 AO1 marks are given. In the second paragraph, each of the attitude components is linked to the example identified in the question — pre-season training — to earn the 3 AO2 marks.
> **6/6 marks awarded**

attitude would be that they believe in the benefits of pre-season training ✓ because it improves your stamina. They would also have positive emotions. Their affective attitude is that they enjoy taking part in pre-season training ✓. Finally, they would demonstrate positive actions. Their behavioural attitude component would show that they attend every training session in pre-season ✓.

Student B

The attitude components are
- cognitive ✓
- associative
- behavioural ✓

This means that they will go to pre-season, enjoy it and believe how good it is for them.

Student B has given an answer that is too brief, and there is little evidence to show that the attitude components are understood. They have correctly identified two out of the three attitude components, although bullet-point answers are not recommended. Student B has also made the common mistake of identifying the second component as 'associative' rather than 'affective'. Associative refers to the second stage of learning. If you read through your answers you should notice these types of error. No AO2 points have been credited. The final sentence of the answer is too vague. Although it might suggest some knowledge of the components, it is not clear which one is being described.
2/6 marks awarded

Question 19

What is cognitive dissonance and how can it be used to change a negative attitude into a positive attitude?

[4 marks]

This requires you to demonstrate that you understand what cognitive dissonance is. There will be 1 mark allocated to this. The other 3 marks are available for the explanation of how to change a negative attitude into a positive one. The best answers will clearly show how each attitude component can be changed.

Student A

Cognitive dissonance is creating a psychological 'unease' in a performer that challenges at least one of their three attitude components ✓. This can mean that the cognitive, affective or behavioural components are disputed, which might instigate a change in the performer's attitude. The cognitive component can be challenged by a significant other giving clear information, so that the performer's thoughts/beliefs are addressed and hopefully changed ✓. The affective component can be challenged by ensuring that the performer has a positive and varied experience ✓. By having an enjoyable and successful time, their confidence and motivation are increased and therefore they have more positive feelings. The affective component, which relates to emotions/feelings, can be changed. Finally, you can change the behavioural component by using persuasive communication ✓ to convince the individual to change their actions and participate. You can persuade them to take part.

Student A approaches this question effectively. A clear definition of cognitive dissonance is given. Each of the three attitude components is then addressed in turn, with an explanation of how it can be changed.
4/4 marks awarded

Student B

The cognitive component of an attitude relates to the performer's thoughts/beliefs. The affective component is the performer's feelings/emotions. The behavioural component is the performer's actions. Cognitive dissonance means that you challenge one of these attitude components by questioning it ✓. If all three attitude components are not aligned then an attitude can be changed.

Student B has misunderstood and/or misread the question. They have accurately described the cognitive, affective and behavioural components, but as they have not described how each component can be changed, no marks are awarded. The definition of cognitive dissonance is creditworthy. **1/4 marks awarded**

Individual differences: motivation

Question 20

Athletes receive a range of rewards in order to motivate them. Describe the types of tangible and intangible rewards that a javelin thrower may receive.　　[4 marks]

This requires you to demonstrate that you know the difference between tangible and intangible rewards and show how a javelin thrower can receive both. Ensure that you refer to the javelin thrower and no other practical examples.

Student A

Tangible rewards are physical ✓ rewards that you can touch. The javelin thrower receives a gold medal ✓ for winning. Intangible rewards are invisible — they cannot be seen or felt. They are not physical ✓. They might include the praise ✓ the javelin thrower receives from their coach when they throw a personal best distance.

This succinct answer correctly describes tangible and intangible rewards that a javelin thrower might receive. **4/4 marks awarded**

Student B

Tangible rewards are things you can touch ✓. Intangible rewards are things you cannot ✓.

A footballer might receive a medal or hear supportive shouts from the stands.

Student B understands the difference between tangible and intangible rewards and has given brief answers that gain credit. However, the examples given relate to a footballer rather than a javelin thrower and therefore are not credited. **2/4 marks awarded**

Individual differences: arousal

Question 21

Using a practical example, describe the catastrophe theory of arousal.　　[4 marks]

This requires you to demonstrate that you understand catastrophe theory and are able to apply this to a sporting example. It is useful to be able to draw and fully label the diagram of this theory, to focus your answer. There will be a sub-max applied to this style of question — if you do not give an example, you will not be able to access all the marks available, even if you offer four correct theory points.

Student A

The catastrophe theory is multidimensional. It considers both psychological and physiological effects on the performer. As arousal increases, so does performance quality ✓ up to an optimum point at moderate arousal ✓, as shown by the inverted-U theory. Once the moderate level of arousal has been exceeded then there is a dramatic decrease in performance as a result of high cognitive anxiety combined with high somatic anxiety ✓. A hockey player is experiencing fatigue towards the end of a cup fixture. They feel extremely worried about the result and are also experiencing negative physical responses such as increased muscle tension. As their optimum arousal level is exceeded, they experience a catastrophe and commit a foul by striking a member of the opposition with their stick, and cannot focus on the game. They cannot do the basics, such as passing or dribbling ✓. Their body and mind have become over-aroused, causing an immediate decline in performance — the catastrophe. If they are able to relax, the effects of the catastrophe can be reversed.

This answer accesses all the available marks. It clearly describes the catastrophe theory and how there is an instant and significant decline in performance once the optimum arousal levels have been exceeded. Student A has given a clear example relating to hockey that illustrates the theory effectively. **4/4 marks awarded**

Student B

The catastrophe theory states that once you exceed the optimum arousal, which is moderate ✓, then performance will drop straightaway ✓. The performer is affected physiologically (somatic) and cognitively (psychological) ✓. If they use relaxation techniques such as deep breathing exercises, then they may be able to continue to perform.

This answer is brief but accesses 3 out of the 4 marks available. It does include a fourth theory point that is correct, but as a sub-max is applied, it will not be credited. In order to access the fourth mark a practical example should be included. **3/4 marks awarded**

Individual differences: anxiety

Question 22

Give a definition of anxiety.   [1 mark]

This straightforward question requires a clear, unambiguous definition. Make sure that you learn and are able to give clear definitions, because these are easy marks to pick up.

Student A

Anxiety is a negative emotion. It causes the performer to experience worry, fear and apprehension ✓.

Student A gives a clear definition of anxiety to access the AO1 mark available. **1/1 mark awarded**

Student B

Anxiety is the level of somatic or cognitive stimulation that gets us ready to perform.

Student B has mistakenly given the definition of arousal instead of anxiety. **0/1 mark awarded**

Question 23

Using practical examples, describe trait and state anxiety. [2 marks]

You have to correctly describe trait and state anxiety *and* give an accurate practical example of each to achieve full marks.

Student A

Trait anxiety means that the performer will feel worried and apprehensive in all situations because it is part of their genetic make-up. For example, whether it is a friendly tennis match or they are taking part in a final, they will feel nervous ✓.

State anxiety is not genetic and therefore it can change from situation to situation. It only happens at specific times. For example, the tennis player might only feel worried when the score is 40/40 ✓. In all other situations they feel confident.

Student A has correctly defined trait and state anxiety and has given clear practical examples to demonstrate knowledge. **2/2 marks awarded**

Student B

Performers with trait anxiety experience feelings of apprehension at all times. It is part of their make-up.

Performers with state anxiety only feel apprehensive and stressed in specific situations. For example, a gymnast experiences state anxiety when they are on the pommel horse, but not on any other piece of apparatus ✓.

Student B has correctly defined trait and state anxiety but is only able to access 1 mark because no practical example of trait anxiety is given. **1/2 marks awarded**

Individual differences: aggression

Question 24

Evaluate the trait theory of aggression. [6 marks]

All 6 marks for this question are for AO3. As the command term is 'evaluate', you must give strengths and weaknesses, advantages and disadvantages, or positives and negatives. Make it clear to the examiner which points are positive and which are negative. There will be a sub-max on this question, which means that there will be a limit on the number of strengths/weaknesses that can be credited. You must give a balanced answer. Although it does not ask specifically for a practical example, it is always useful to offer one to support the theory in your answer.

Student A

The strengths of the trait theory of aggression are that it states that aggression is a natural ✓ part of being a human. Aggression is genetic and if we are provoked enough, we will act aggressively — we cannot stop it from happening, it is inevitable ✓. Once an aggressive act has happened, for example a rugby player strikes out at a defender who has illegally tackled them above the shoulder, then the player will feel better. Their aggression is released. This is known as the cathartic effect ✓.

A weakness of the trait theory is that it completely discounts the social learning theory ✓, resulting in the nature versus nurture debate. It does not accept that aggression can be learned through observation, as suggested by Bandura following his bobo doll experiment. Bandura has shown that people who watch aggressive acts will then imitate them, especially if the person they are watching is a significant other ✓. On the other hand people can watch and copy non-aggressive actions ✓ — according to trait theory this would not be possible. The theory also does not take into account that some individuals and groups of people, such as Buddhists, will never be aggressive even if they are heavily provoked ✓. People may also be aggressive in one environment but not others. For example, when playing ice hockey, an individual comes into contact with an opposing player and immediately responds in an aggressive manner. The same player is contacted by a defender when playing netball but does not react aggressively. According to the trait theory, it would not matter what sport they were playing — they would react aggressively.

Student A clearly understands the trait theory of aggression and is able to evaluate the theory to access the AO3 marks on offer. The answer is balanced and, although it is not required, reference to practical situations is used to strengthen the answer.
6/6 marks awarded

Student B demonstrates some understanding of the trait theory. However, due to the brevity of the answer, only 3 marks are awarded. One strength and two weaknesses of the theory are given. To access all the marks available, offer at least three positive and three negative remarks.
3/6 marks awarded

Student B

The trait theory says that all humans react aggressively because we inherit this instinct from our parents. It also says that because aggression is inherited, we show it consistently ✓. The weaknesses of this theory are that it is quite simple ✓. Also, not everyone acts aggressively ✓.

Social facilitation

Question 25

Using practical examples, explain the effects of an audience on a performer and describe strategies to reduce any negative effects that may occur as a result of the audience being present.

[8 marks]

This question has two parts. To access all of the marks you must ensure that you address both parts in your answer. In the first part you should explain the positive and negative effects that are experienced by a performer when an audience is present. You must also include practical examples to access the AO2 marks. There will be a sub-max of 5 marks available for this section. In the second part of your answer you should describe the cognitive and somatic strategies that you can use to reduce the negative effects on performance when an audience is present.

Student A

Social facilitation refers to the positive and negative effects that a performer experiences when an audience is present. Social facilitation describes the positive effects experienced — their performance gets better. Social inhibition describes the negative effects experienced — their performance worsens.

When an audience is present, they may or may not be actively observing the performer. Regardless of this, if the performer *perceives* that they are being observed, their performance will be affected either positively or negatively.

The first effect that the performer will experience is an increase in their arousal levels ✓. As a result of this the performer will revert back to performing their dominant response ✓. This is a well-learned skill that they use when under pressure. If they are an autonomous performer, for example they are an elite basketballer, the dominant response of a short chest pass is likely to be performed correctly ✓. This is because the performer is experienced and used to performing in front of an audience. If the skill being performed is a simple skill that does not require a lot of decisions to be made (for example, a forward roll) or if the skill is gross, that is, it utilises large muscle groups and does not require a lot of precision, accuracy and control (for example, running), then the skill will be performed accurately. The audience's presence has had a positive effect, and performance is facilitated.

Sometimes the presence of an audience has a negative effect on performance. Cognitive performers, for example a novice gymnast, will not be as successful in front of an audience because they are distracted by it and their arousal levels are heightened ✓. If the skill is complex, for example passing in hockey, then several decisions need to be made. If the skill is fine, for example a pistol shot, which requires precision, accuracy and control, then it may not be performed correctly ✓. The audience's presence has had a negative effect, and performance is inhibited.

To reduce the negative effects of social inhibition, a range of techniques can be used to reduce the performer's arousal levels and therefore enable them to better deal with the audience being present.

Familiarisation training allows the players to train in front of a crowd, so that they get used to it. For example, the coach invites supporters to watch netball training sessions in the lead-up to a big local derby ✓.

The player should selectively attend — focus on the relevant cues and disregard the irrelevant distractions — to reduce the effects of the crowd. For example, when taking a penalty, focus on the ball and target area only and ignore the spectators behind the goal ✓.

This is an excellent response. Student A has clear and detailed knowledge about the positive and negative effects of social facilitation and inhibition. They demonstrate the depth of knowledge required for A-level. The answer is well-structured and uses specialist terminology throughout. Clear and accurate links to practical sporting situations are given throughout. A number of strategies to limit the negative effects are given and again are supported by practical examples. Student A has given more answers than there are marks available, which is good practice.
8/8 marks awarded

The player could utilise cognitive and/or somatic stress management techniques to reduce the effects of an audience being present. For example, a dancer could use mental rehearsal — going over the dance routine in their mind. This is a cognitive strategy. A somatic strategy is progressive muscular relaxation ✓. This is when the performer focuses on their muscle groups and, working from top to bottom, they tense and release each muscle group in turn. Finally, the coach should offer encouragement to increase self-confidence when performing in front of an audience, for example shouting 'well done' when the performer does correct footwork in netball.

Student B

Being watched can make you do better or worse. Experienced performers can do better; new performers will do worse. Zajonc suggested that there were passive and interactive others. You can use visualisation to help you go over the tackle in your head ✓. This links to drive theory.

This answer is too brief and shows limited understanding. The statements made are vague and there is insufficient detail in the answer to allow Student B to access any more marks. There appears to be some understanding about how the performer's stage of learning impacts on their ability to deal with the presence of an audience, but this has not been explained clearly enough to gain credit. Although Zajonc's model is relevant, there needs to be an explanation as to how passive audiences affect performers. There is no explanation of how this links to drive theory. **1/8 marks awarded**

Group and team dynamics in sport

Question 26

Identify the four stages of group formation according to Tuckman. Put a tick (✓) in the box next to the correct answer.

[1 mark]

A   Norming, warming, forming, roaming

B   Forming, storming, norming, performing

C   Forming, norming, performing, modelling

D   Forming, norming, adjourning, storming

The question requires you to know the four stages specifically. Read the question carefully so that mistakes are not made.

Student A

A   Norming, warming, forming, roaming

B   Forming, storming, norming, performing   ✓

C   Forming, norming, performing, modelling

D   Forming, norming, adjourning, storming

Student A has accurately identified B as the correct answer and has marked it with a tick. **1/1 mark awarded**

Student B

A Norming, warming, forming, roaming	
B Forming, storming, norming, performing	✓
C Forming, norming, performing, modelling	✓
D Forming, norming, adjourning, storming	

The student has identified the correct answer but has also ticked an incorrect answer. The examiner will only accept one answer, so this cannot be credited because it is unclear which of the answers Student B thinks is correct.
0/1 mark awarded

Question 27

How can a coach increase the cohesiveness of their team? [4 marks]

The question requires you to show how a coach creates unity in their team. Your answer should say what the coach does, not what the players do.

Student A

The coach should develop both task and social cohesion by making sure that the players they pick are the ones that work together the best, rather than just picking good individuals who play for themselves rather than the team ✓. The coach should also praise the team when they work together as a unit to achieve the team's goal ✓. The coach should also make sure that all the squad wears the team's hoodies/training kit when travelling to fixtures because this gives them a collective identity ✓. During pre-season, the coach should organise a team-building day, such as Go Ape, so they get to know each other and become friends ✓. If everyone knows their specific roles and duties in the team, that will also help to bring them together.

This excellent answer gives ways to develop both task and social cohesion. Student A also gives more correct answers than marks available, which is good exam technique.
4/4 marks awarded

Student B

A cohesive team has a clear structure and a common goal, and its members all work together to reach it. Cohesive teams are more successful.

Student B has misread the question and given a definition. Make sure you read everything before you answer a question. Student B obviously has some understanding of this area of the specification but has given away marks by not reading the question properly.
0/4 marks awarded

Goal setting in sports performance

Question 28

Outline the benefits of setting goals. [3 marks]

This requires you to state the benefits, but not the principles or types, of goal setting.

Student A

Setting goals keeps you motivated ✓ and increases confidence ✓. It also controls arousal levels ✓.

> This is short, sharp and to the point.
> **3/3 marks awarded**

Student B

A performer can set process, performance or outcome goals. Process goals aim to improve technique, performance goals aim to improve from last time and outcome goals aim to win.

> Student B has misunderstood the question and described the types of goal that can be set rather than the benefits of goals. Read the question carefully. **0/3 marks awarded**

Attribution

Question 29

A netball coach asks the wing attack to play out of position and take on the goal attack role for the first time against a top-level goal defence. The team loses the fixture and the player experiences a loss of confidence. With reference to Weiner's model, describe the attributions that the player may give.

[4 marks]

> This requires solid knowledge and understanding of Weiner's model. There are four attributions and each one will be allocated 1 mark. To achieve each mark, link the attribution to the netball goal attack.

Student A

Attributions are the reasons that the netballer gives when they win or lose.

Weiner suggested that there are four main attributions — ability, task difficulty, effort and luck. The locus of causality says that attributions can be internal or external. Internal attributions such as ability and effort are within the netballer's control. For example, the netballer might say that the team lost due to ability; this is because the player believes that they do not have the coordination or perceptual ability to play in the goal attack role ✓. They might also think that the rest of the team did not believe the player could play well in goal attack and therefore they did not put the effort in, and because the player does not like playing there, they did not put in as much effort as normal either ✓.

External attributions such as task difficulty and luck are outside of the netballer's control. The task was made more difficult for the player because they were playing against an experienced goal defence when this was the first time they had played as goal attack ✓. The player might also suggest that some of the umpire's decisions were incorrect. For example, the player was unlucky to be punished for bad footwork ✓.

The stability dimension describes how permanent the attributions are. Stable reasons such as ability and task difficulty remain the same. This is the perceived low ability of the netballer who thinks they are just not able to succeed in the goal attack position; and also the difficult task of playing against a tough and experienced goal defence. Unstable attributions such as effort and luck can change from minute to minute and game to game. For example, at the beginning of the match the player put a lot of effort in, trying to move into space quickly. Towards the end of the match the player did not put as much effort in and therefore did not score as many goals. Luck also changes — the netballer hit the ring on several occasions rather than scoring.

Student A has accessed all the available marks. Through the description of the locus of causality and the stability dimension, they have clearly demonstrated understanding of Weiner's model of attribution. For each of the four attributions, Student A has linked the theory to the practical example in the question.
4/4 marks awarded

Student B

Weiner says that ability, effort and luck can be given as attributions. Luck is when the referee gives the 50/50 decision your way when it is not clear who headed the ball into touch. Ability can be given as the reason for losing if the netballer thinks they are simply not good enough and do not have the coordination, speed or power needed to score goals ✓. They then do not put any effort in.

Student B has given a brief answer. Only three attributions are listed rather than four — task difficulty has been missed out. The example given relating to luck refers to the skill of heading, which is not a skill used in netball. Ensure that you read the question carefully. If a specific skill/example is referred to in the question, you must use this in your answer. Other examples will not be credited. The reference to effort is not clarified and therefore is not credited. **1/4 marks awarded**

Confidence and self-efficacy in sports performance

Question 30

Explain Bandura's model of self-efficacy. Use practical examples to illustrate your answer.   [4 marks]

This relies on your knowledge of Bandura's model of self-efficacy. Bandura has other models in other areas of the specification, so make sure you explain the correct one. Each of the 4 marks on offer can be accessed by giving the theory and a relevant practical example.

Student A

Bandura's model states that self-efficacy is influenced by four factors — performance accomplishments, vicarious experiences, verbal persuasion and emotional arousal. Performance accomplishments mean that a coach can remind a netballer who is being moved out of position from wing attack to goal attack of when they were successful before. For example, the coach might recap the results of a shooting drill when the netballer was 100% accurate with their shots ✓. This has the greatest effect on the performer according to Bandura, and raises self-efficacy most readily.

Vicarious experiences describe how the coach highlights other performers completing the same task successfully. In this case, the coach might show the netballer videos of their teammate who made the transition from a wing position to shooter successfully ✓. If this player shares characteristics with the netballer, for example gender/age/ability, then this will have a bigger impact on the netballer.

Verbal persuasion is about the coach encouraging the netballer. The coach should praise the netballer for accurate passing, shooting and overall effectiveness as a goal attack ✓. The encouragement from the coach will raise the self-efficacy of the netballer.

Emotional arousal requires the performer to understand and control their arousal/stimulation levels. The netballer will have heightened arousal levels because they are playing out of position. The netballer should perform stress management techniques such as mental rehearsal and progressive muscular relaxation to control their arousal levels when playing as a goal attack ✓ and therefore increase self-efficacy.

> Student A scores full marks on this answer which clearly demonstrates understanding of Bandura's model of self-efficacy. For each of the four parts of the model, the student has described what is required to increase the performer's self-efficacy and this is then linked to a practical example. **4/4 marks awarded**

Student B

Bandura's model states that self-efficacy can be developed through performance accomplishments, vicarious persuasion, motor reproduction and emotional arousal. Performance accomplishments refer to the individual recalling previous successes. Vicarious persuasion is giving the performer positive reinforcement. Emotional arousal is helping the performer to lower their stress and anxiety. If all of these are in place, then self-efficacy will increase.

> Student B gains no credit for this answer. Performance accomplishments and emotional arousal are correctly identified as part of the model, but there is no practical example to illustrate either of these, so these answers score no marks. Student B has incorrectly referred to vicarious persuasion. Two parts of the model are vicarious experiences and verbal persuasions. Finally, motor reproduction is not part of Bandura's model of self-efficacy; it is part of Bandura's observational learning theory. **0/4 marks awarded**

Leadership in sport
Question 31

What is the difference between a prescribed leader and an emergent leader? Give a practical example to illustrate where each can be found in sport.

[4 marks]

> This question has 2 AO1 marks on offer for the descriptions of prescribed and emergent leaders. There are also 2 AO2 marks on offer for the practical applications. Ensure that you address both aspects of the question.

Student A

Emergent leaders occur when the group members themselves select their captain, coach or leader from inside their own team ✓. For example, a volleyball team selects its captain because they are the most experienced player and have been the key motivator ✓.

Prescribed leaders are chosen and then appointed from outside the group ✓. For example, the FA selected Phil Neville as the manager of the England women's football team ✓.

> Student A accesses all of the marks available. Both types of leadership are clearly defined, and the answer is supported with accurate sporting examples. **4/4 marks awarded**

> Student B has mixed up the definitions so cannot access the AO1 marks, and has not offered any practical examples, so the AO2 marks are immediately lost. In the pressure of the exam it is easy to make silly mistakes like this. To avoid them, make sure you leave up to 5 minutes at the end to read all of your answers. This mistake could have been spotted and remedied quickly.
> **0/4 marks awarded**

Question 32

Using a practical example to illustrate your answer, explain Chelladurai's multidimensional model of leadership.
Analyse which leadership styles are most appropriate for different performers.*

[10 marks]

> This is an extended synoptic question that requires you to draw together the multidimensional model of leadership and also leadership styles. You need to access as many AO1, AO2 and AO3 marks as you can. Remember that this is a banded mark question, so your answer is assessed holistically. One correct answer does not mean 1 mark. Show your knowledge and understanding of Chelladurai's model and apply each point of the model to a practical example. It is highly likely that you will be provided with an image of the model as part of the question, but it is not guaranteed and therefore make sure that you can recall the model if needed. If you are not given the model, spend a short amount of time sketching it as part of your plan because this will help you to focus your answer.
>
> The second part of the question requires you to analyse which leadership styles are most appropriate to use for different individuals. Do not forget this part of the question. Remember that your quality of written communication is also assessed as part of the answer, so write in full sentences and use the correct terminology.

Student A

Chelladurai suggested that leaders should be adaptable to a variety of situations AO1. A leader's aim should be to gain high-quality performances and high levels of satisfaction AO1 from the team that they are leading. In other words, through effective leadership the team will perform at its best and it members will feel happy about being part of the team. This increases the cohesiveness of the team and is known as the consequences of effective leadership. This is an excellent way to address leadership. Too often coaches are stuck in their old ways and do not change, even if the team does not respond well to the approach they are taking.

In order to increase the performance quality and satisfaction of the team, the leader should consider the antecedents AO1 before deciding which leadership style would be most appropriate. The situational characteristics include the level of danger AO2, strength of opponents AO2, facilities AO2 and time available AO2.

Using the example of rock-climbing AO2, the situation is dangerous and therefore a leader should recognise that an autocratic approach would be most appropriate. An autocratic leader is someone who is task-orientated. Their main concern is completing the task and they make all the decisions personally. They are dictatorial in style. This means they give an order and you follow it. This is an effective style of leadership as the job gets done quickly. This would be the most appropriate style for an outdoor and adventurous activity such as rock-climbing. The leader would have to give clear instructions to ensure the safety of all involved. Male performers AO3 prefer this style of leadership. It is also necessary for cognitive performers AO3, but when a group is cohesive then autonomous performers AO3 may also opt for this style.

The leader should also consider the group member AO1 characteristics. Groups do not like change and therefore their traditions should be carefully taken into account. If their previous leader was a democrat and the new leader acts autocratically, this may cause hostility and in-fighting, and therefore lower the performance and satisfaction of the group AO3. Their ability and level of experience AO1 should also be considered. If, for example, the group comprises cognitive rock-climbers AO2, it is obviously best to lead autocratically, instructing them clearly on how to belay and where to place their hands and feet in order for them to develop their skills quickly and efficiently AO2. Gender and age are also issues because females AO3 and older AO3 performers prefer to work under democratic leadership. These two demographic groups like to have their opinions heard, while males prefer autocratic training and instruction AO3.

Another consideration would be the leader's characteristics, including their personality, ability and preferred style of leadership AO1. They may be quite a timid person and dislike being authoritarian, thus preferring a democratic leadership style AO2. In the case of the cognitive rock-climbers, this style would not be the most appropriate to choose and therefore the group may not feel satisfied, lowering performance levels AO2. If the leader preferred to adopt an authoritarian, autocratic style because it suited their ability and personality then there would be a high level of congruence with the other factors, resulting in higher performance and satisfaction from the group AO2.

Once the leader has considered these three factors, they can begin to decide which style would be most appropriate to use to lead the group successfully. They must also take into account the required behaviour AO1. This is dictated by the situation AO1 because the leader must analyse what style of leadership is needed. For example, in rock-climbing the situation requires a high level of direction to maintain safety AO2. Therefore the style that would be most congruent with the requirements would be the autocratic style AO2.

The group members dictate the preferred behaviour AO1. This is the style they like best and is often based, as stated before, on tradition, ability and gender AO2. In the example of the rock-climbers, if as a group they liked autocratic best and the leader acted autocratically then they would feel happy and satisfied, resulting in an improvement in performance levels AO2.

The actual leader behaviour relates to the style of leadership adopted by the leader AO1. Once they have considered the five factors above, they must try to match their style to the various requirements set by the group — what they prefer, as well as the situation and what it needs. If there is a high degree of congruence, then the performance and satisfaction levels will increase AO1.

To conclude, in the rock-climbing example the situation demands that an autocratic style is adopted AO2. This is set by the required behaviour AO1. The group, being novices, would need an autocratic leader in order to develop their skills AO2. This is probably preferred by the group too because they will progress quickly AO3. They would learn the basics of climbing in a short amount of time AO2. If the leader decides then to adopt an autocratic approach regardless of any personal preference, then the group would be happy, satisfied and would show a higher level of performance AO2.

Should the leader choose to disregard all the factors and lead in a manner that suits them personally rather than what the group needs and wants, then inevitably the performance level of the group will decrease as they will not be satisfied AO2. This might ultimately motivate them to leave the group, or lead to a vote of no confidence in the leader, and therefore a new leader must be appointed AO2.

This excellent level-3 answer shows that Student A has detailed knowledge and understanding of Chelladurai's model. Every part of the model is described effectively and supported by an example relating to leading a group of rock-climbers. Throughout the answer, a high level of specialist terminology is used. It is well-structured, and the quality of written communication is high. The second part of the question is addressed and analyses which leadership style is most appropriate for a range of performers, with reference to their gender and ability level. Student A accesses a range of AO1, AO2 and AO3 marks. **10/10 marks awarded**

Student B

Chelladurai's model is used to show how different leadership styles can be employed. The situation AO1, the leader AO1 and the group AO1 should all be considered before deciding how to lead. The leader's behaviour is also affected by the required behaviour and the behaviour that is liked the best. The leader needs to work out what the situation needs and if their own leadership style is suited to this, then this would work better for the group. If the situation is white-water rafting AO2, it needs a firm, autocratic leader AO2. If the required behaviour is laissez-faire and this is the style that the group likes the best, then this is the style that the leader should try. This could be used in dance when the group members know what they are doing and therefore do not really need a leader and just do the routine on their own AO2.

Question 33

Describe the autocratic and laissez-faire styles of leadership styles. [6 marks]

To access all 6 marks available in this question, you must give at least three correct descriptions of the autocratic style and three correct descriptions of the laissez-faire style of leadership. A sub-max will be applied to ensure that your answer is balanced.

Student A

The autocratic style of leadership means the leader is focused on getting the task in hand completed ✓. The autocratic leader will be the sole decision maker ✓ and will not consult their team. They are described as being dictators ✓.

Laissez-faire leaders are just figure-heads. They allow the group to make all the decisions ✓ and offer little, if any, feedback to the group ✓. This style can only be used effectively if the group members are autonomous ✓.

Student B

Autocratic leaders use a command style ✓ of leadership as they are dictators ✓. They are not concerned about developing personal relationships with the group members ✓ and they work as quickly as possible to get the job done.

Laissez-faire leaders do very little. The group members do as they please ✓.

This weak level-1 answer achieves 3 marks at the most. Even though 3 AO1 and 3 AO2 points have been accessed, the knowledge and understanding demonstrated are only satisfactory. Some parts of the model have been identified but not explained. Descriptions of 'required behaviour' and 'preferred behaviour' have been attempted but are too vague to be credited. Student B has only limited success with using the specialist, technical vocabulary of the model. The answer is relatively basic and unstructured. Examples of white-water rafting and dance are referred to, but it would have been better to keep the same example throughout and apply it to each part of the model. No AO3 points have been credited because there is no reference to the second part of the question. You must ensure that all parts of the question are attempted in order to access all the marks on offer. **3/10 marks awarded**

Student A has given an accurate and balanced answer. They have clearly described both styles of leadership and therefore accessed all the marks on offer. **6/6 marks awarded**

Student B has fallen foul of the 'sub-max' rule and has therefore missed out on 2 marks. They have given four credit-worthy answers about autocratic leaders but only one in the laissez-faire section. Once the examiner has given 3 marks for autocratic leaders, the sub-max has been hit and the remaining 3 marks must come from the laissez-faire section. Make sure your answers are balanced. **4/6 marks awarded**

Stress management to optimise performance
Question 34

A footballer is asked to take a penalty kick. What negative cognitive and somatic effects might they experience? [4 marks]

> The question requires you to apply your knowledge. Ensure that you include the cognitive and somatic effects that a footballer experiences when taking a penalty.

Student A

The footballer might experience cognitive effects such as negative thoughts ✓ that they might miss the goal and feel extremely worried ✓. They might also fear the reaction of the crowd. They might notice somatic effects such as an increase in heart rate and blood pressure ✓ when doing the run up, as well as increased sweating ✓.

> Full credit is given because the answer describes both cognitive and somatic effects. **4/4 marks awarded**

Student B

- Shakes
- Fear of failure
- Stress

> Basic bullet-point answers such as these are too brief and lack the necessary detail. There is also no link to the footballer/penalty situation, as required by the question.
> **0/4 marks awarded**

Knowledge check answers

1 Continuity is based on the clarity of the start and end of the movement and how closely linked the subroutines are.

Difficulty is based on the amount of information to process and, as a result, the level of decision-making and perception/judgements required to produce the skill.

2 The organisation and complexity of the skill; the level of danger involved; the clarity of the start and end; the environment

3 Part, whole, whole-part-whole, progressive-part, massed, distributed, fixed, varied

4 The effect that the learning and performance of one skill may have on the learning and performance of another

5 Positive transfer is when the learning and performance of one skill helps the athlete to learn and perform another skill.

Negative transfer is when the learning and performance of one skill hinders the athlete when learning and performing another skill.

6 Proactive transfer, which can be positive or negative, occurs when the learning and performance of a current skill has an effect on a future skill.

Retroactive transfer, which can be positive or negative, occurs when the learning and performance of a skill has an effect on a skill that has been learned and performed previously.

7 Law of readiness, law of exercise, law of effect

8 Saying nothing when the successful action is shown following a period of criticism

9 The whole is greater than the sum of its parts; kinaesthesis and flow of the skill are maintained.

10 Attention, retention, motor reproduction, motivation

11 Advantages: can be given immediately, useful for open skills, used effectively in conjunction with visual guidance, used to give autonomous performers technical and tactical information

Disadvantages: information overload may occur, performer may lose concentration, cognitive performers may not understand the technical terms

12 Intrinsic, extrinsic, positive, negative, knowledge of performance, knowledge of results

13 Correct errors, prevent incorrect actions reoccurring, avoid development of bad habits, reinforce correct actions, improve performer's confidence and motivation

14

Extroverts	Introverts
Like social situations	Dislike social situations
Are outgoing	Are reserved
Like performing with an audience	Dislike performing in front of an audience
Become bored easily because the RAS is not easily stimulated	Are easily over-aroused because the RAS is easily stimulated

15 Cognitive, affective, behavioural

16 Social learning, socialisation, past experiences, reinforcement

17 Cognitive dissonance involves generating unease inside the individual in order to change one or more of the negative attitude components into positive ones.

18 Intrinsic — from within the performer
Extrinsic — from an outside source

19 The dominant response is a well-learned skill that the performer will revert to when under competitive pressure.

20 Moderate

21 High cognitive anxiety combined with high somatic anxiety

22 Cognitive anxiety — psychological symptoms
Somatic anxiety — physiological symptoms

23 Catharsis is a feeling of calm that is experienced as a result of releasing negative emotions.

24 An aggressive cue is a trigger that is present that increases the likelihood of an aggressive act occurring.

25 Social facilitation — performance improves when being watched by an audience
Social inhibition — performance worsens when being watched by an audience

26 Evaluation apprehension is the fear of being judged.

27 Two or more people, interaction, a common goal, mutual awareness, collective identity

28 Forming, storming, norming, performing

29 actual productivity = potential productivity – losses due to faulty processes

30 Specific, Measurable, Achievable, Recorded, Time-phased

31 Ability, task difficulty, effort, luck

32 Global — general/relating to all sports
Specific — relating to a single sport or skill within a sport

33 Self-confidence — a generalised feeling of assurance that you have the ability to meet demands; an absence of doubt
Self-efficacy — how much belief you have in your ability to achieve goals. It is the belief that you can be successful when carrying out a particular/specific task.

34 SC-state is the level of confidence in a particular situation — often based on past experience.

35 Performance accomplishments, vicarious experiences, verbal persuasion, emotional arousal

36 Prescribed leaders are chosen from outside the group. Emergent leaders are selected from within the group, often nominated by the other group members.

37 Autocratic, democratic, laissez-faire

38 Stress is a negative response that causes anxiety. Eustress is a positive response to a threat, which is seen as a challenge to overcome.

39 Cognitive effects of stress are psychological.
Somatic effects of stress are physiological.

Note: **bold** page numbers refer to definitions.